W9-CQQ-342

Namo Fundamental Teacher Shakyamuni Buddha

"Until the hells are empty,
I vow not to become a Buddha;
Only after all living beings are saved,
will I myself attain Bodhi."

Earth Store Bodhisattva

Sutra of
the
Past Vows
of
Earth Store Bodhisattva

Sutra of
the
Past Vows
of
Earth Store Bodhisattva

Translated into Chinese by the
Tripitaka Shramana Shikshananda of Udyana

English translation by the
Buddhist Text Translation Society

Buddhist Text Translation Society
Dharma Realm Buddhist University
Dharma Realm Buddhist Association
Burlingame, California U.S.A.

Sutra of the Past Vows of Earth Store Bodhisattva

Published and translated by:
Buddhist Text Translation Society
1777 Murchison Drive, Burlingame, CA 94010-4504

© 2014   **Buddhist Text Translation Society**
Dharma Realm Buddhist University
Dharma Realm Buddhist Association

Buddhist Text Translation Society
4951 Bodhi Way, Ukiah, CA 95482
www.buddhisttexts.org
info@buddhisttexts.org

First edition 1982
Second edition 2003
Thrd edition 2014

ISBN 978-1-60103-047-4 (third edition hardcover)
ISBN 978-1-60103-048-1 (first edition ebook)

Printed on non-acid paper in Malaysia

Library of Congress Cataloging-in-Publication Data

Library of Congress Cataloging-in-Publication Data

Tripitaka. Sutrapitaka. Ksitigarbhasutra. English.
    Sutra of the Past Vows of Earth Store Bodhisattva / Translated into Chinese by the Tripitaka Shramana Shikshananda of Udyana ; English translation by the Buddhist Text Translation Society. -- Third edition.
    pages cm
Previously published: 2003.
ISBN 978-1-60103-047-4 (hardcover : alk. paper) --
ISBN 978-1-60103-048-1 (ebook)
I. Siksananda, 652-710. II. Buddhist Text Translation Society. III. Title.

BQ1712.E5B83 2014
294.3'85--dc23

2014002051

The Eight Guidelines of
The Buddhist Text Translation Society

1. A volunteer must free him/herself from the motives of personal fame and profit.

2. A volunteer must cultivate a respectful and sincere attitude free from arrogance and conceit.

3. A volunteer must refrain from aggrandizing his/her work and denigrating that of others.

4. A volunteer must not establish him/herself as the standard of correctness and suppress the work of others with his or her fault-finding.

5. A volunteer must take the Buddha-mind as his/her own mind.

6. A volunteer must use the wisdom of Dharma-selecting Vision to determine true principles.

7. A volunteer must request Virtuous Elders in the ten directions to certify his/her translations.

8. A volunteer must endeavor to propagate the teachings by printing and distributing Sutras, Shastra texts, and Vinaya texts when the translations are certified as being correct.

Contents

Incense Praise
Verse for Opening a Sutra

The True Words of Seven Buddhas
   for Eradicating Offenses
Spirit Mantra for Rebirth in the Pure Land
Mantra for Patching the Flaws in Recitation
Praise
Earth Store Bodhisattva Praise

The True Words of Seven Buddhas
   for Eradicating Offenses
Spirit Mantra for Rebirth in the Pure Land
Mantra for Patching the Flaws in Recitation
Praise
Earth Store Bodhisattva Praise
Verse of Transference

Incense Praise

Incense in the censer now is burning;

All the Dharma Realm receives the fragrance,

From afar the sea vast host of Buddhas all inhale
its sweetness.

In every place auspicious clouds appear,

Our sincere intention thus fulfilling,

As all Buddhas now show their perfect bodies.

Namo Incense Cloud Canopy Bodhisattva,
Mahasattva. (3X)

Namo Fundamental Teacher Shakyamuni Buddha.

Verse for Opening a Sutra

The unsurpassed, profound, and wonderful Dharma,

Is difficult to encounter in hundreds of millions of eons.

I now see and hear it, receive and uphold it,

And I vow to fathom the Tathagata's true meaning.

Part One

of

Sutra of the Past Vows of Earth Store Bodhisattva

CHAPTER I

Spiritual Penetrations in the Palace of the Trayastrimsha Heaven

Thus I have heard. At one time, the Buddha was in the Trayastrimsha Heaven speaking Dharma for his mother. At that time, ineffable, ineffable, Buddhas and Great Bodhisattvas Mahasattvas from infinite worlds in the ten directions assembled to praise Shakyamuni Buddha's ability to manifest inconceivable great wisdom and powerful spiritual penetrations in the evil world of the Five Turbidities. They lauded his ability to regulate and subdue obstinate living beings so that these beings would come to know the Dharma of suffering and bliss. Each one sent his attendants to pay their respects to the World Honored One.

At that time, the Thus Come One smiled and emitted billions of great light-clouds, such as the light-cloud of great perfection, the light-cloud of great compassion, the light-cloud of great wisdom, the light-cloud of great *prajna*, the light-cloud of great samadhi, the light-cloud of great auspiciousness, the light-cloud of great blessings, the light-cloud of great merit, the light-cloud of great refuge, and the light-cloud of great praise.

After emitting all of these indescribable light-clouds, he also emitted many wonderful subtle sounds, such as the *dana paramita* sound, *shila paramita* sound, *kshanti paramita* sound, *virya paramita* sound, *dhyana paramita* sound, and *prajna paramita* sound. There was the sound of compassion, the sound of joyous giving, the sound of liberation, the sound of no outflows, the sound of wisdom, the sound of great wisdom, the sound of the Lion's roar, the sound of the Great Lion's roar, the sound of thunderclouds, and the sound of great thunderclouds.

After such indescribable sounds had been emitted, countless millions of gods, dragons, ghosts, and spirits from the Saha and other worlds also gathered in the Palace of the Trayastrimsha Heaven.

They came from the Heaven of the Four Kings, the Trayastrimsha Heaven, the Suyama Heaven, the Tushita Heaven, the Blissful Transformations Heaven, and the Heaven of Comfort Gained through Others' Transformations.

They came from the Heaven of the Multitudes of Brahma, the Heaven of the Ministers of Brahma, the Heaven of the Great Brahma Lord, the Heaven of Lesser Light, the Heaven of Limitless Light, the Heaven of Light Sound, the Heaven of Lesser Purity, the Heaven of Limitless Purity, and the

Heaven of Universal Purity.

They came from the Birth of Blessings Heaven, the Love of Blessings Heaven, the Abundant Fruit Heaven, the No Thought Heaven, the No Affliction Heaven, the No Heat Heaven, the Good Views Heaven, the Good Manifestation Heaven, the Ultimate Form Heaven, the Maheshvara Heaven, and so forth to the Heaven of the Station of Neither Thought nor Non-Thought.

All those groups of gods, dragons, ghosts and spirits came and gathered together.

Moreover, sea spirits, river spirits, stream spirits, tree spirits, mountain spirits, earth spirits, brook and marsh spirits, sprout and seedling spirits, day, night, and space spirits, heaven spirits, food and drink spirits, grass and wood spirits, and other such spirits from the Saha and other worlds came and gathered together.

In addition, all the great ghost kings from the Saha and other worlds came and gathered together. They were: the ghost king Evil Eyes, the ghost king Blood Drinker, the ghost king Essence and Energy Eater, the ghost king Fetus and Egg Eater, the ghost king Spreader of Sickness, the ghost king Collector of Poisons, the ghost king Kindhearted, the ghost king Blessings and Benefits, the ghost king Great Regard and Respect, and others.

At that time, Shakyamuni Buddha said to the Dharma Prince Manjushri Bodhisattva Mahasattva, "As you regard these Buddhas, Bodhisattvas, gods, dragons, ghosts, and spirits from this world and other worlds, from this land and other lands who are now gathered in the Trayastrimsha Heaven, do you know how many of them there are?"

Manjushri said to the Buddha, "World Honored One, even if I were to measure and reckon with my spiritual powers for a thousand eons, I would not be able to know how many of them there are."

The Buddha told Manjushri, "Regarding them with my Buddha eye, I also cannot count them all. Those beings have been taken across, are being taken across, will be taken across, have been brought to accomplishment, are being brought to accomplishment, or will be brought to accomplishment by Earth Store Bodhisattva throughout many eons."

Manjushri said to the Buddha, "World Honored One, I have cultivated good roots for a long time and have certified to unobstructed wisdom. When I hear what the Buddha says, I immediately accept it with faith. But Hearers of small attainment, gods, dragons, and the rest of the eightfold division, and beings in the future, who hear the Thus Come One's true words, will certainly harbor doubts. Even if they receive the teaching most respectfully, they will still be unable to avoid slandering it. My only wish is that the World Honored One will proclaim for everyone what Earth Store Bodhisattva Mahasattva practiced and what vows he made while on the level of planting causes that now enable him to accomplish such inconceivable deeds."

The Buddha said to Manjushri, "By way of analogy, suppose that each blade of grass and tree in a field or forest, each rice plant, hemp stalk, bamboo, reed, and each dust mote from mountain boulders in a Three Thousand Great Thousand World System were a Ganges River. Then suppose that each grain of sand in each of those Ganges Rivers were a world and that each dust mote in each of those worlds were an eon. Then suppose each dust mote accumulated in each of those eons was itself an eon. The time elapsed since Earth Store Bodhisattva was certified to the position of the Tenth Ground is a thousand times longer than that in the above analogy. Even longer was the time he dwelled on the levels of Hearer and Pratyekabuddha.

"Manjushri, the awesome spiritual vows of this Bodhisattva are inconceivable. If good men or women in the future hear this Bodhisattva's name, praise him, behold or bow to him, call his name, make offerings to him, or if they draw, carve, cast, sculpt, or paint images of him, such people will be reborn in the Heaven of the Thirty-Three one hundred times and will never fall into the evil paths.

"Manjushri, ineffable ineffable eons ago, during the

time of a Buddha named Lion Sprint Complete in the Ten Thousand Practices Thus Come One, Earth Store Bodhisattva Mahasattva was the son of a great elder. That elder's son, upon observing the Buddha's hallmarks and fine features and how the thousand blessings adorned him, asked that Buddha what practices and vows had endowed him with such hallmarks. Lion Sprint Complete in the Ten Thousand Practices Thus Come One then said to the elder's son, 'If you wish to have a body like this, you must, throughout long eons, liberate all living beings who are undergoing suffering.'

"Manjushri, that comment caused the elder's son to make a vow: 'From now until the end of future time throughout uncountable eons, I will use expansive expedient means to help beings in the six paths who are suffering for their offenses. Only when they have all been liberated, will I myself become a Buddha.' From the time he made that great vow in the presence of that Buddha until now, hundreds of millions of *nayutas* of ineffable eons have passed, yet he is still a Bodhisattva.

"Another time, inconceivable *asamkhyeya* eons ago, there was a Buddha named Enlightenment-Flower Samadhi Self-Mastery King Thus Come One. That Buddha's life span was four hundred billion *asamkhyeya* eons. During his Dharma-Image Age, there lived a Brahman woman who was endowed with many blessings from previous lives and who was respected by everyone. Whether she was walking, standing, sitting, or lying down, gods surrounded and protected her. Her mother, however, embraced a deviant faith and often slighted the Triple Jewel.

"The worthy daughter made use of many expedients in trying to convince her mother to hold right views, but her mother never totally believed. Before long, the mother's life ended and her consciousness fell into the Relentless Hell.

"When her mother's life ended, the Brahman woman, knowing that her mother had not believed in cause and effect while alive, feared that her karma would certainly pull her into the evil paths. For that reason, she sold the family house and procured vast quantities of incense, flowers, and various other items and performed a great offering in that Buddha's stupa and temple. In one of the temples, she saw an especially fine and majestic image of the Thus Come One Enlightenment-Flower Samadhi Self-Mastery King.

As the Brahman woman beheld the Honored One's countenance, she became doubly respectful and thought to herself, 'A Buddha is called Greatly Enlightened One Endowed with All-Wisdom. If this Buddha were in the world, I could ask him where my mother went after she died. He would certainly know.'

"The Brahman woman then wept for a long time as she gazed longingly upon the Thus Come One. Suddenly a voice in the air said, 'O weeping worthy woman, do not be so sorrowful. I shall now show you where your mother has gone.'

"The Brahman woman placed her palms together as she said into space, 'Which divinity is comforting me in my grief? From the day I lost my mother, I have held her in memory day and night, but there is nowhere I can go to ask about the realm of her rebirth.'

"The voice in the air spoke to the woman again, 'I am the one you behold and worship, the former Enlightenment-Flower Samadhi Self-Mastery King Thus Come One. Because I have seen your regard for your mother is double that of ordinary beings, I have come to show you where she is.'

"The Brahman woman suddenly raised herself and lunged toward the voice she was hearing; she then fell, injuring all her limbs. Those around her supported and attended to her, and after a long time she was revived. Then she addressed the air saying, 'I hope the Buddha will be compassionate and quickly tell me into what realm my mother has been reborn. I am now near death myself.'

"Enlightenment-Flower Samadhi Self-Mastery King Thus Come One told the worthy woman, 'After you make your offerings, return home quickly. Sit upright and concentrate on my name. You will soon know where your mother has been reborn.' The Brahman woman bowed to the Buddha and returned home. The memory of her mother sustained her as she sat upright recollecting Enlightenment-Flower Samadhi Self-Mastery King Thus Come One.

"After doing so for a day and a night, she suddenly saw herself beside a sea whose waters seethed and bubbled. Many dreadful beasts with iron bodies were pursuing each other swiftly back and forth above the sea. She saw billions of men and women bobbing up and down in the sea, being fought over, seized, and eaten by those beasts. She saw *yakshas* with different forms. Some had many hands, some many eyes, some many legs, and some many heads. With their protruding fangs sharp as swords, they drove the offenders on towards those beasts. Furthermore, the beasts and yakshas seized the offenders and twisted their heads and feet together into shapes so horrible that no one would dare even look at them for long.

"During that time the Brahman woman was naturally without fear due to the power of recollecting the Buddha.

"A ghost king named Poisonless came, bowed his head in greeting and said to the worthy woman, 'Welcome, O Bodhisattva. What conditions bring you here?'

"The Brahman woman asked the ghost king, 'What is this place?'

"Poisonless replied, 'We are on the western side of the Great Iron Ring Mountain and this is the first of the seas that encircle it.'

"The worthy woman asked, 'I have heard that the hells are within the Iron Ring. Is that actually so?'

"Poisonless answered, 'Yes, the hells are here.'

"The worthy woman asked, 'How have I now come to the hells?'

"Poisonless answered, 'If it wasn't awesome spiritual strength that brought you here, then it was the power of karma. Those are the only two ways that anyone can come here.'

"The worthy woman asked, 'Why is this water seething and bubbling, and why are there so many offenders and dreadful beasts?'

"Poisonless replied, 'These are beings of Jambudvipa who did evil deeds. They have just died and passed through forty-nine days without any surviving relatives doing any meritorious deeds on their behalf to rescue them from their distress. Moreover, during their lives they themselves didn't plant any good causes. Hence their own karma calls forth these hells. They must, of course, cross this sea first. Ten thousand *yojanas* east of this sea is another sea in which they will undergo twice as much suffering. East of that sea is yet another sea where the sufferings are doubled yet again. What the combined evil causes of the three karmas evoke are all called the sea of karma. This is that place.'

"The worthy woman asked the Ghost King Poisonless, 'Where are the hells?'

"Poisonless answered, 'Within the three seas are hundreds of thousands of great hells, each one different. Eighteen of those are known as the great hells. Five hundred subsequent ones inflict limitless cruel sufferings. Following those are hundreds of thousands that inflict limitless further sufferings.'

"The worthy woman again questioned the great ghost king, 'My mother died recently and I do not know where her spirit has gone.'

"The ghost king asked the worthy woman, 'When the Bodhisattva's mother was alive, what deeds did she do?'

"The worthy woman replied, 'My mother held wrong views and ridiculed and slandered the Triple Jewel. Even if she occasionally believed, she would soon become disrespectful again. She died recently and I still do not know where she was reborn.'

"Poisonless asked, 'What was the Bodhisattva's mother's name and clan?'

"The worthy woman replied, 'My parents were both Brahmans; my father's name was Shila Sudarshana, my mother's name was Yue Di Li.'

"Poisonless placed his palms together and implored the worthy woman, 'Please, Worthy One, quickly return home. There is no need for you to grieve further. The offender Yue Di Li was born in the heavens three days ago. It is said that she received the benefit of offerings made and blessings cultivated by her filial child who, for her mother's sake, practiced giving at the stupas and temples of Enlightenment-Flower Samadhi Self-Mastery King Thus Come One. Not only was the Bodhisattva's mother released from the hells, but all the other offenders who were in the Relentless Hell also received bliss and were reborn together with her.' Having finished speaking, the ghost king put his palms together and withdrew.

"The Brahman woman returned swiftly as if from a dream, understood what had happened, and then made a profound and far-reaching vow before the stupas and images of Enlightenment-Flower Samadhi Self-Mastery King Thus Come One, saying, 'I vow that, until the end of future eons, I will respond to beings suffering for their offenses by using many expedient devices to bring about their liberation.'"

The Buddha told Manjushri, "The Ghost King Poisonless is the present Bodhisattva Foremost Wealth. The Brahman woman is now Earth Store Bodhisattva."

CHAPTER II

The Division Bodies Gather

At that time, the division bodies of Earth Store Bodhisattva began gathering in the palace of the Trayastrimsha Heaven from all the hells in the billions of inexpressible, inconceivable, immeasurable, ineffable, limitless *asamkhyeyas* of worlds.

Due to the spiritual powers of the Thus Come One, each came from his own direction and was joined by thousands of billions of *nayutas* of those who had attained liberation from the path of karma. All brought incense and flowers as offerings to the Buddha.

Those groups that came were irreversible from *Anuttarasamyaksambodhi* because they had been taught by Earth Store Bodhisattva.

For long eons they had wandered in birth and death, undergoing suffering within the six paths without even temporary respite. Now they had reached various levels of sagehood, due to the great compassion and deep vows of Earth Store Bodhisattva.

They felt joyful as they arrived at the Trayastrimsha Heaven and gazed at the Thus Come One, their eyes not leaving him for a moment.

At that time, the World Honored One stretched forth his golden-colored arm and rubbed the crowns of all the division bodies of Earth Store Bodhisattva Mahasattva gathered from billions of inexpressible, inconceivable, immeasurable, ineffable, limitless *asamkhyeyas* of worlds, and said, "I teach obstinate beings such as these within the evil worlds of the five turbidities, causing their minds to be regulated and subdued so they renounce the improper and return to the proper. But one or two of ten still cling to their bad habits. For them I again divide into billions of bodies and use numerous expedient means. Those with keen roots will listen and immediately believe. Those with good rewards will respond to exhortation and strive to succeed. Those who are dim and dull will return only after being taught for a long time. Those whose karma is heavy fail to show any respect.

"My division bodies take across and liberate all those different kinds of beings. I may appear as a man, a woman, a god or dragon, a spirit or ghost. I may appear as a mountain, a forest, a stream, a plain, a river, a lake, a fountain, or a well in order to benefit people, so they would all be liberated. I may appear as God Shakra, Lord Brahma, a wheel-turning king, a lay person, a king, a prime minister, an official, a Bhikshu, a Bhikshuni, an Upasaka, an Upasika, a Hearer, an Arhat, a Pratyekabuddha, or a Bodhisattva in order to teach and rescue beings. It is not that I only appear to them as a Buddha.

"Reflect on how I have toiled for many eons and endured much hardship to take across and free those stubborn and difficult beings who are suffering from their offenses. Those not yet subdued undergo retributions according to their karma. If they fall into the evil destinies and are undergoing tremendous suffering, then you should remember the gravity of this entrustment I am now making to you here in the palace of the Trayastrimsha Heaven: find ways to liberate all beings in the Saha world from now until the time when Maitreya comes into the world; help them escape suffering forever, encounter Buddhas, and receive predictions."

At that time, all the division bodies of Earth Store Bodhisattva that came from all those worlds merged into a single form. Then he wept and said to the Buddha, "Throughout long eons, I have been receiving the Buddha's guidance and from that have developed inconceivable spiritual power and great wisdom. My division bodies fill worlds as many as grains of sand in millions of billions of Ganges Rivers. In each of those worlds, I transform myself into millions of billions of bodies. Each body rescues millions of billions of people, helping them to return respectfully to the Triple Jewel, escape birth and death forever, and reach the bliss of Nirvana. Even if their good deeds within the Buddhadharma amount to as little as a strand of hair, a drop of water, a grain of sand, or a mote of dust, or the tip of a hair, I will gradually take them across, liberate them, and help them gain great benefit. I only hope that the World Honored One will not be worried about beings of the future who have bad karma."

In that way he addressed the Buddha three times: "I only hope that the World Honored One will not be worried about beings of the future who have bad karma."

At that time, the Buddha praised Earth Store Bodhisattva and said, "Excellent! Excellent! I will help you in this work you so willingly undertake. When the vast vows that you keep making throughout so many eons are fulfilled and all those beings have been saved, then you will be certified as having attained Bodhi."

CHAPTER III

Contemplating the Karmic Conditions of Beings

At that time, the Buddha's mother, Lady Maya, placed her palms together respectfully and asked Earth Store Bodhisattva, "Great Sage, could you tell us about the different kinds of karma that beings of Jambudvipa create, and the resulting retributions that they undergo?"

Earth Store replied, "There are millions of worlds and lands that may or may not have hells, may or may not have women, may or may not have the Buddhadharma, and so forth to having or not having Hearers and Pratyekabuddhas. Since the worlds differ, the retributions in the hells also differ."

Lady Maya spoke again to the Bodhisattva, "Could you please tell us about the offenses done by those in Jambudvipa that result in retributions in the evil destinies?"

Earth Store replied, "Worthy Mother, please listen as I speak briefly about that."

The Buddha's mother answered, "Great Sage, please do tell us about it."

Then Earth Store Bodhisattva said to the worthy mother, "Retributions that result from offenses committed in Jambudvipa are described like this:

"Beings who are not filial to their parents, even to the point of harming or killing them, will fall into the Relentless Hell where, for thousands of billions of eons, they will seek escape in vain.

"Beings who shed the Buddha's blood, slander the Triple Jewel, and do not venerate sutras will fall into the Relentless Hell where, for thousands of billions of eons, they will seek escape in vain.

"Beings who usurp or damage the property of the Eternally Dwelling, who defile Bhikshus or Bhikshunis, who commit sexual acts within the Sangharama, or who kill or harm beings will fall into the Relentless Hell where, for thousands of billions of eons, they will seek escape in vain.

"Beings who seem to be Shramanas but in their minds are not Shramanas, who destroy the things of the Eternally Dwelling, who deceive lay people, who go against the precepts, and who do many other evil deeds will fall into the Relentless Hell where, for thousands of billions of eons, they will seek escape in vain.

"Beings who steal the wealth and property of the Eternally Dwelling, including its grains, food and drink, and clothing, or who take anything at all that was not given to them, will fall into the Relentless Hell where, for thousands of billions of eons, they will seek escape in vain."

Earth Store continued, "Worthy Mother, beings who commit such offenses will fall into the fivefold relentless hell where they will constantly seek temporary relief from their suffering but will never receive even a moment's relief."

Lady Maya further asked Earth Store Bodhisattva, "Why is that hell called Relentless?"

Earth Store replied, "Worthy Mother, the hells are all within the Great Iron Ring Mountain. The eighteen great hells and the five hundred subsequent ones each have their own name. There are hundreds of thousands more that also have their own names. The Relentless Hell is found within a city of hells that encompasses more than eighty thousand square miles. That city is made entirely of iron and is ten thousand miles in height, with an unbroken mass of fire above it. Within the city are many interconnected hells, each with a different name.

"There is just one hell called Relentless. Its circumference is eighteen thousand miles. The wall of that hell is a thousand miles high, totally made of iron, and covered with a fire burning downward that is joined by a fire burning upward. Iron snakes and dogs spewing fire race back and forth atop that wall.

"In that hell is a bed that extends for ten thousand miles. One person undergoing punishment perceives his or her own body covering the entire bed. When hundreds of thousands of people undergo punishment simultaneously, each still perceives his or her own body covering the bed. That is how retributions are undergone by those with the same karma.

"What is more, these offenders undergo extreme suffering. Hundreds of thousands of *yakshas* and other evil ghosts display fangs like swords and eyes like lightning as they pull and drag the offenders with their brass-clawed hands.

Other *yakshas* wield huge iron halberds that they use to pierce the offenders' mouths and noses or stab their bellies and backs. They toss the offenders into the air and then catch them by skewering them with the halberds, or they let them drop onto the bed. Iron eagles peck at the offenders' eyes and iron serpents wrap around their necks. Long nails are driven into all their joints. Their tongues are pulled out, stretched, and then plowed through. Their internal organs are gouged out, sliced, and minced. Molten metal is poured into their mouths, and their bodies are bound with hot iron. Responses to their karma go on like that throughout thousands of deaths and rebirths. They pass through hundreds of millions of eons seeking escape in vain.

"When this world is destroyed, they find themselves in another world. When that world is destroyed, they pass on to another one. When that world, too, is destroyed, they move on to another. When this world comes into being again, they return here. The situation involving Relentless retribution for offenses is like that.

"Moreover, five karmic responses account for the name Relentless. What are the five?

First, it is said to be Relentless because punishment is undergone day and night throughout many eons without ceasing for a moment.

Second, it is said to be Relentless because one person fills it in the same way that many people fill it.

"Third, it is said to be Relentless because repeated punishments continue without cease throughout years that stretch into *nayutas* of eons. Those punishments are inflicted by instruments of torture such as forks and clubs; or by eagles, serpents, wolves, and dogs; or by pounding, grinding, sawing, drilling, chiseling, cutting and chopping; or by boiling liquids, iron nets, iron ropes, iron donkeys, and iron horses; or by rawhide strips bound around one's head and molten iron poured over one's body; or by meals of iron pellets and drinks of molten iron.

"Fourth, it is said to be Relentless because all beings undergo karmic responses based on the offenses that they have committed, whether they be men, women, savages, old, young, honorable, or lowly; whether they be dragons, spirits, gods, or ghosts.

"Fifth, it is said to be Relentless because offenders continually undergo ten thousand deaths and as many rebirths each day and night from the moment they first enter this hell and on through hundreds of thousands of eons. During that time if they seek even a moment's relief it never comes. Only when their karma is exhausted can they leave the hell and be born elsewhere."

Earth Store Bodhisattva said to the worthy mother, "That is a brief description of the Relentless Hell. If I were to speak extensively about the names of all the implements of punishment in the hells and all the sufferings there, I could not finish speaking in an entire eon."

After hearing that, Lady Maya placed her palms together sorrowfully, made obeisance, and withdrew.

CHAPTER IV

Karmic Retributions of Beings of Jambudvipa

At that time Earth Store Bodhisattva Mahasattva said to the Buddha, "World Honored One, because I receive the awesome spiritual strength of the Buddha, Thus Come One, I am able to divide my body and rescue beings who are undergoing karmic retributions everywhere in billions of worlds. If it were not for the great compassionate strength of the Thus Come One, I would be unable to manifest such transformations. Now the World Honored One has entrusted me with rescuing and liberating beings in the six paths until Ajita becomes a Buddha. I accept the entrustment, World Honored One. Please have no further concern."

Then the Buddha told Earth Store Bodhisattva, "Beings who have not yet attained liberation have unstable natures and perceptions. Their bad habits reap bad karma; their good habits bring rewards. Reacting to situations by doing good or evil deeds causes them to turn in the five paths without a moment's rest. Confused and beset by troubles, they pass through eons as numerous as dust motes.

Like fish swimming through waters laced with nets, they may slip through and keep their freedom temporarily, but, sooner or later, they will be caught. I am concerned about such beings. But, since you keep making extensive vows repeatedly throughout successive eons to take such offenders across, what further worries need I have?"

After that was said, a Bodhisattva Mahasattva in the assembly named Samadhi Self-Mastery King said to the Buddha, "World Honored One, what vows has Earth Store Bodhisattva made during so many successive eons that now cause him to receive the World Honored One's repeated praise? We hope the World Honored One will briefly tell us about this."

Then the World Honored One replied to Samadhi Self-Mastery King, "Listen attentively, listen attentively, and reflect well as I now explain the details for you. One time, limitless *asamkhyeyas* of *nayutas* of ineffable eons ago, a Buddha named All-Knowledge-Accomplished Thus Come One, One Worthy of Offerings, One of Proper and Pervasive Knowledge, One Perfect in Clarity and Conduct, Well-Gone One, Unsurpassed Knight Who Understands the World, Taming and Subduing Hero, Teacher of Gods and Humans, Buddha, World Honored One, appeared in the world. That Buddha's life span was sixty thousand eons. Before he became a monk, he was the king of a small country and was friendly with the king of a neighboring country. Both kings practiced the ten wholesome deeds and benefited beings. Because the citizens of those two neighboring countries did many bad things, the two kings made a plan using far-reaching expedients. One king vowed to quickly become a Buddha and then rescue all the others.

"The other king vowed, 'I do not want to become a Buddha until I first rescue all those who are suffering for their offenses, enabling them to find peace and finally to reach Bodhi.'"

The Buddha told the Bodhisattva Samadhi Self-Mastery King, "The king who vowed to quickly become a Buddha is All-Knowledge-Accomplished Thus Come One. The king who vowed to keep saving beings who are suffering for their offenses rather than become a Buddha is Earth Store Bodhisattva.

"Another time, limitless asamkhyeya eons ago, a Buddha named Pure-Lotus-Eyes Thus Come One appeared in the world. His life span was forty eons. In his Dharma-Image Age, an Arhat who taught beings as he encountered them, rescuing them by letting them create blessings, once met a woman named Bright Eyes, who offered a meal to him.

"'What is your wish?' asked the Arhat.

"Bright Eyes replied, 'On the day of my mother's death, I

performed meritorious deeds to rescue her, but I do not know into what path my mother has been reborn.'

"Sympathizing with her, the Arhat entered samadhi to contemplate and saw that Bright Eyes' mother had fallen into a bad destiny where she was undergoing extreme suffering. The Arhat asked, 'Bright Eyes, what did your mother do while alive that make her have to now undergo such terrible suffering in a bad destiny?'

"Bright Eyes replied, 'My mother enjoyed eating fish, turtles, and other sea creatures. She indulged in eating fried or broiled fish and turtle eggs, taking lives that numbered in the millions. Oh, Venerable One, please be compassionate and tell me how she can be saved!'

"The Arhat took pity on Bright Eyes, used his skillful means, and urged Bright Eyes thus, 'With sincere resolve, be mindful of Pure-Lotus-Eyes Thus Come One and also make carved and painted images of him. When you do, both the living and the dead will be rewarded.'

"On hearing this, Bright Eyes renounced everything she loved, and swiftly commissioned painted images of the Buddha. Then she made offerings before them. She wept sorrowfully as she respectfully beheld and bowed to the Buddha. Suddenly, during the second half of the night, in a dream, she saw that Buddha's body - dazzling gold in color and as large as Mount Sumeru - emitting great light.

"That Buddha said to Bright Eyes, 'Your mother will be born in your household before long and as soon as that infant can feel hunger and cold, he will speak.'

"Shortly thereafter, a maidservant in the house bore a son who spoke before he was three days old. Lowering his head and weeping, he said to Bright Eyes, 'The karmic conditions we create during our lives and deaths result in retributions that we ourselves must undergo. I was your mother and have been in darkness for a long time. Since you and I parted, I have repeatedly fallen into the great hells. Upon receiving the power of your blessings, I have been reborn as a person of low station with a short life span. Thirteen years from now, I will fall into the evil paths again. Do you have some way to free me so that I can avoid them?'

"When Bright Eyes heard those words, she knew without a doubt that they were her mother's. Choked with sobs, she said to the servant's child, 'Since you were my mother, you should know your own past offenses. What karma did you create that caused you to fall into the evil paths?'

"The maidservant's child answered, 'I am undergoing retribution for two kinds of karma: killing and slandering. Had I not received the blessings you earned to rescue me from difficulty, I would not yet be released from that karma.'

"Bright Eyes asked, 'What happens in the hells when beings undergo retribution for their offenses?

"'The maidservant's son answered, 'I can't bear to speak of the ways in which beings suffer for their offenses. Even in a hundred thousand years, I would find it hard to finish describing it.'

"When Bright Eyes heard that, she wept bitterly and spoke into the air, saying, 'I vow that my mother will be released from the hells forever. At the end of these thirteen years, she will be done with her heavy offenses and will not go back to the evil paths. O Buddhas of the ten directions, with your compassion and sympathy, please listen to the vast and mighty vow that I am making for the sake of my mother. If my mother will never again enter the three evil paths, will never again be born into low stations, and will never again be a woman, then here before the image of Pure-Lotus-Eyes Thus Come One, I vow that from this day on, throughout millions of billions of eons, I will respond to all beings who are undergoing suffering for their offenses in the hells or the three evil paths of any world. I vow to rescue them from the bad destinies of the hells, hungry ghosts, animals, and the like. Only after beings with such retributions have all become Buddhas will I myself achieve Proper Enlightenment.'

"After making that vow, she clearly heard Pure-Lotus-Eyes Thus Come One say to her, 'Bright Eyes, your own great compassion and sympathy will reach your mother through this mighty vow that you are making. My contemplation shows me that after thirteen years your mother will be done with this retribution and will be born a Brahman with a life span of one hundred years. After that retribution, she will be born in the Land of No Concern with a life span of uncountable eons. Later she will realize the fruition of Buddhahood and save people and gods as numerous as sand grains in the Ganges.'"

Shakyamuni Buddha told Samadhi Self-Mastery King, "The Arhat who bestowed blessings and helped Bright Eyes then is now Inexhaustible Intention Bodhisattva. The mother of Bright Eyes is now Liberation Bodhisattva. Bright Eyes herself is now Earth Store Bodhisattva. He has been extending his compassion and sympathy like that from distant eons onward by making vows as many as Ganges' sands to rescue vast numbers of beings.

"Men and women in the future may fail to do good deeds and only do evil; may not believe in cause and effect; may indulge in sexual misconduct and false speech; may use divisive and harsh speech; and may slander the Great Vehicle. Beings with karma like that should certainly fall into bad destinies. But if they encounter Good and Wise Advisors who exhort them and lead them to quickly take refuge with Earth Store Bodhisattva, then those beings will just as quickly be released from their retributions in the three evil paths. If those beings are determined and respectful, if they behold, bow to, and praise the Bodhisattva, and if they make offerings of flowers, incense, clothing, jewels, food, and drink to him, they will enjoy supremely wonderful bliss in the heavens for millions of billions of eons. When their blessings in the heavens end and they are born as people, throughout hundreds of thousands of eons, they will often be national leaders able to remember all aspects of causes and effects from previous lives. O Samadhi Self-Mastery King, Earth Store Bodhisattva has such inconceivable great awesome spiritual power that he uses expansively for the benefit of beings. All of you Bodhisattvas should remember this sutra, and proclaim and spread it far and wide."

Samadhi Self-Mastery King said to the Buddha, "World Honored One, please do not be concerned. We billions of Bodhisattvas Mahasattvas, based on the Buddha's awesome spiritual strength, will certainly proclaim this sutra widely throughout Jambudvipa for the benefit of beings."

Having spoken thus to the World Honored One, Samadhi Self-Mastery King Bodhisattva put his palms together respectfully, bowed, and withdrew.

At that time, the Four Heavenly Kings rose from their seats, placed their palms together respectfully, and said to the Buddha, "World Honored One, Earth Store Bodhisattva has been making such great vows from distant eons past until now. Why is it that even now he has not yet finished taking beings across? Why does he continue to renew his vast and mighty vows? Please, World Honored One, explain that for us."

The Buddha told the Four Heavenly Kings, "Excellent, excellent. Now, to bring benefit to you and to extend that benefit to people and gods of the present and future, I will speak about how Earth Store Bodhisattva, out of compassion and pity, uses expedient devices, within the paths of birth and death in Jambudvipa in the Saha world, to rescue, take across, and liberate beings who are undergoing suffering for their offenses."

The Four Heavenly Kings replied, "Please, World Honored One, we would like to hear about his work."

The Buddha told the Four Heavenly Kings, "From distant eons past up to the present, Earth Store Bodhisattva has been rescuing and liberating beings. Since his vows are still not fulfilled, he continues with compassion and sympathy to help beings suffering for their offenses in this world. Moreover, he sees the ceaseless tangle of their causes extending on through infinite future eons. Because of that, he renews his vows. Thus, in this Saha world, on the continent of Jambudvipa, this Bodhisattva teaches and transforms beings by means of millions of billions of expedient devices.

"O Four Heavenly Kings! To killers, Earth Store Bodhisattva speaks of the retribution of a short life span. To robbers, he speaks of the retribution of the acute suffering of poverty. To those who indulge in improper sex, he speaks of the retribution of rebirth as sparrows or as mandarin drakes or ducks. To those who use harsh speech, he speaks of the retribution of quarrelling families.

"To those who slander, he speaks of the retribution of being without a tongue and having a cankerous mouth. To the hateful, he speaks of the retribution of being ugly and disabled. To the stingy, he speaks of the retribution of not getting what they seek. To gluttons, he speaks of the retribution of hunger, thirst and sicknesses of the throat. To those who hunt without restraint, he speaks of the retribution of dying a terrifying, violent death.

"To those who are unfilial to their parents, he speaks of the retribution of being killed in natural disasters. To arsonists who burn mountains and forests, he speaks of the retribution of going insane and losing their own lives.

"To cruel parents or stepparents, he speaks of the retribution of being flogged in future lives. To those who net and trap animals, he speaks of the retribution of being separated from one's own children or parents. To those who slander the Triple Jewel, he speaks of the retribution of being blind, deaf, or mute. To those who slight the Dharma and regard the teachings with contempt, he speaks of the retribution of remaining in the bad paths forever. To those who destroy or misuse possessions of the Eternally Dwelling, he speaks of the retribution of revolving in the hells for hundreds of millions of eons. To those who defile the pure conduct of others and bear false witness against members of the Sangha, he speaks of the retribution of remaining in the animal realm forever. To those who scald, burn, dismember, maim, or otherwise harm beings, he speaks of the retribution of undergoing the very same suffering.

"To those who violate precepts and the regulations of pure eating, he speaks of the retribution of being born as birds or beasts that must suffer hunger. To those who make reckless and destructive use of things, he speaks of the retribution of being unable to ever obtain what they seek. To the arrogant and haughty, he speaks of the retribution of being servile and of low station. To those who use backbiting to cause discord among others, he speaks of the retribution of being without a tongue or having speech impediments. To those with misguided views, he speaks of the retribution of being reborn in backward regions.

"The bad habits involving body, mouth, and mind karma

that beings of Jambudvipa perpetuate, result in hundreds of thousands of retributions like those. I have only listed a few examples here. Since the varying karma created by beings of Jambudvipa brings about different responses, Earth Store Bodhisattva uses hundreds of thousands of expedient means to teach and transform beings. Those beings must first undergo retributions such as those, and then fall into the hells, where they pass through eons without being able to escape. You should therefore protect people and protect nations. Do not allow the various kinds of karma to confuse beings."

On hearing that, the Four Heavenly Kings wept in sorrow, placed their palms together, and withdrew.

End of Part One of

Sutra of the Past Vows of Earth Store Bodhisattva.

The True Words of Seven Buddhas for Eradicating Offenses

li po li po di, qiu he qiu he di, tuo luo ni di,
ni he la di, pi li ni di, mo he qie di,
zhen ling qian di, suo po he. (3x)

Spirit Mantra for Rebirth in the Pure Land

na mo e mi duo po ye, duo tuo qie duo ye,
duo di ye tuo, e mi li du po pi, e mi li duo,
xi dan po pi, e mi li duo, pi jia lan di,
e mi li duo, pi jia lan duo, qie mi li,
qie qie nuo, zhi duo jia li, suo po he. (3x)

Mantra for Patching the Flaws in Recitation

na mo he la da na, duo la ye ye,
qie la qie la, ju zhu ju zhu, mo la mo la,
hu la, hong, he he su da na, hong, po mo nu,
suo po he. (3x)

Praise

The Thus Come One, out of kindness and pity,

Turns the great Dharma Wheel;

The Brahma woman kindly saves her kin;

Enlightenment Flower takes beings across
      the stream of confusion;

And Lady Maya asks Earth Store Bodhisattva
      about causes.

Homage to Earth Store Bodhisattva Mahasattva. (3x)

Earth Store Bodhisattva Praise

Earth Store Bodhisattva, wonderful beyond compare;

Gold-hued in his transformation body he appears.

Wondrous Dharma-sounds throughout the
    Three Paths and Six Realms;

Four Births and Ten Kinds of Beings gain his kindly grace.

His pearl, shining brightly, lights the way to heaven's halls;

Six-ringed golden staff shakes open wide the gates of hell.

Leads on those with causes garnered life and life again;

To bow at the Nine-flowered Terrace of
    the Honored One.

Namo Earth Store Great Vows and Compassion

Bodhisattva of the dark and dismal worlds;

On Nine Flower Mountain, Most Honored One,

With Ten Wheels of power you rescue all
    the suffering ones.

Homage to Earth Store Bodhisattva.
(Recite while circumambulating)

Part Two

of

Sutra of the Past Vows of Earth Store Bodhisattva

CHAPTER V

The Names of the Hells

At that time, Universal Worthy Bodhisattva Mahasattva said to Earth Store Bodhisattva, "Humane One, for the sake of gods and dragons, those in the fourfold assembly, and all other beings of the present and future, please tell us the names of the hells where beings in the Saha world on the continent of Jambudvipa must suffer retributions for offenses they commit. Please also describe what happens during retributions undergone for evil deeds, so that beings in the future Dharma-Ending Age will know what those retributions are."

Earth Store Bodhisattva replied, "Humane One, based on the awesome spiritual power of the Buddha and relying on your strength, Great Lord, I will give a general list of the names of the hells and describe some of what happens during retributions undergone for offenses and evil deeds.

"Humane One, in eastern Jambudvipa there is a mountain range called Iron Ring. The mountain is pitch black because the light of the sun and moon does not shine on it. A great hell named Ultimately Relentless is located there. Another hell is called Great Avichi. There is also a hell called Four Corners, a hell called Flying Knives, a hell called Fiery Arrows, a hell called Squeezing Mountains, a hell called Piercing Spears, a hell called Iron Carts, a hell called Iron Beds, a hell called Iron Oxen, a hell called Iron Clothing, a hell called Thousand Blades, a hell called Iron Donkeys, a hell called Molten Copper, a hell called Embracing Pillar, a hell called Flowing Fire, a hell called Plowing Tongues, a hell called Hacking Heads, a hell called Burning Feet, a hell called Pecking Eyes, a hell called Iron Pellets, a hell called Quarrelling, a hell called Iron Ax, and a hell called Massive Hatred."

Earth Store Bodhisattva said, "Humane One, within the Iron Ring are endless hells like that. There is also the hell of Crying Out, the hell of Pulling Tongues, the hell of Dung and Urine, the hell of Copper Locks, the hell of Fire Elephants, the hell of Fire Dogs, the hell of Fire Horses, the hell of Fire Oxen, the hell of Fire Mountains, the hell of Fire Rocks, the hell of Fire Beds, the hell of Fire Beams, the hell of Fire Eagles, the hell of Sawing Teeth, the hell of Flaying Skin, the hell of Drinking Blood, the hell of Burning Hands, the hell of Burning Feet, the hell of Hanging Hooks, the hell of Fire Rooms, the hell of Iron Cells, and the hell of Fire Wolves.

"Each of those hells contains lesser hells numbering from one, or two, or three, or four, to hundreds of thousands. Each of those lesser hells has its own name."

Earth Store Bodhisattva told Universal Worthy Bodhisattva, "Humane One, such are the karmic responses of beings in Jambudvipa who commit evil deeds. The power of karma is extremely great. It rivals Mount Sumeru in its height. It surpasses the great oceans in its depth. It obstructs the path leading to sagehood. For that reason, beings should never think that minor bad deeds are unimportant or assume that they do not count as offenses. After death, there will be retributions to undergo that reflect all those details. Fathers and sons have the closest relationship, but their roads diverge and each must go his own way. Even if they met, neither would consent to undergo suffering in the other's place. Now, based on the awesome spiritual power of the Buddha, I will describe some of the retributions for offenses that take place in the hells. Please, Humane One, listen for a moment to what I am going to say."

Universal Worthy replied, "I have long known of the retributions that come about in the three evil paths. My hope in asking the Humane One to describe them is that when beings in the future Dharma-Ending Age who are committing evil deeds hear the Humane One's descriptions, they will be moved to take refuge with the Buddha."

Earth Store said, "Humane One, this is what happens during retributions in the hells. Offenders may go to a hell in which their tongues are stretched out and plowed through by cattle; or to a hell in which their hearts are pulled out and eaten by yakshas; or to a hell in which their bodies are cooked in cauldrons of boiling liquid; or to a hell in which they are forced to embrace red-hot copper pillars; or to a hell in which they are burned by a massive fire that constantly pursues them; or to a hell that is always ice-cold; or to a hell in which excrement and urine are endless; or to a hell full of flying balls covered with spikes; or to a hell in which fiery spears stab them repeatedly; or to a hell in which objects are constantly ramming into their chests and backs; or to a hell in which their hands and feet are burned; or to a hell in which they are bound by iron snakes that coil around them; or to a hell in which they are pursued by racing iron dogs; or to a hell in which their bodies are stretched by iron mules.

"Humane One, to inflict these retributions in each hell, hundreds of thousands of instruments made of copper, iron, stone, or fire arise from karmic forces. Those four materials come into being in response to the kinds of karma that offenders create. If I were to explain in detail what happens during retributions in the hells, then I would need to tell of the hundreds of thousands of sufferings that must be undergone in each specific hell. How much more would that be the case for the sufferings in all the many hells! Now, having based myself upon the awesome spiritual power of the Buddha, I have given a general answer to the Humane One's question, for if I were to speak in detail, I would not finish for eons."

CHAPTER VI

The Thus Come One's Praises

At that time the World Honored One emitted a great bright light from his entire body, totally illuminating Buddhalands as many as grains of sand in billions of Ganges Rivers. His strong voice reached all the Bodhisattvas Mahasattvas in those Buddhalands, as well as the gods, dragons, ghosts and spirits, humans, non-humans, and others, as he said, "Listen today, as I praise Earth Store Bodhisattva Mahasattva, who displays an inconceivable awesome spiritual strength and compassionate power throughout the ten directions as he rescues and protects beings who are suffering for offenses they have committed. After I pass into tranquility, all of you Bodhisattvas, Great Lords, and all of you gods, dragons, ghosts, spirits, and others should use vast numbers of expedient means to protect this sutra and to cause all beings to testify to the bliss of Nirvana."

After that was said, a Bodhisattva in the assembly named Universally Expansive placed his palms together respectfully and said to the Buddha, "Today we have witnessed the World Honored One praising Earth Store Bodhisattva's inconceivable great awesome spiritual virtue. We hope the World Honored One will also aid beings in the future Dharma-Ending Age by telling us how Earth Store Bodhisattva benefits people and gods and about the workings of cause and effect. That will help the gods, dragons, and the rest of the eightfold division, along with beings of the future, to receive the Buddha's teaching respectfully."

At that time, the World Honored One said to the Bodhisattva Universally Expansive and to all those in the fourfold assembly, "Listen attentively, listen attentively. I will briefly describe to you how Earth Store Bodhisattva's virtuous deeds keep benefiting people and gods."

Universally Expansive replied, "Certainly, World-Honored One. We will gladly listen."

The Buddha told the Bodhisattva Universally Expansive, "If, in the future, good men or good women, upon hearing Earth Store Bodhisattva Mahasattva's name, place their palms together, praise him, bow to him, or gaze at him in worship, they will overcome thirty eons' worth of offenses. Universally Expansive, if good men or women gaze upon and bow but once to painted or drawn images of the Bodhisattva or ones made of clay, or stone, or lacquer, or gold, or silver, or bronze, or iron, they will be reborn one hundred times in the Heaven of the Thirty-Three and will eternally avoid falling into the evil destinies. If their blessings in the heavens come to an end and they are born in the human realm, they will become national leaders who suffer no loss of benefits.

"There may be women who dislike having female bodies. Suppose they wholeheartedly make offerings to images of Earth Store Bodhisattva, such as paintings or images made of clay, or stone, or lacquer, or brass, or iron or other materials. If they continually make such offerings, day after day without fail, of flowers, incense, food, drink, clothing, colored silks, banners, money, jewels, and other items as offerings, then when those good women finish their current female retributions, throughout thousands of millions of eons they will never again be born in worlds where there are women, much less be one, unless it be through the strength of their compassionate vows, in order to liberate beings. Based on the strength of their offerings to Earth Store Bodhisattva and the power of their meritorious virtues, they will not be born into female bodies for hundreds of thousands of eons.

"Moreover, Universally Expansive, some women may have imperfect features or be prone to sickness. Disliking those problems, they can sincerely gaze at and bow to images of Earth Store Bodhisattva with sincere resolve for even just a few minutes, and consequently, throughout millions of future eons of rebirth, they will continually be endowed with full and perfect features. If those women whose features are currently imperfect do not dislike having female bodies, then throughout millions of billions of lives they will always be born as women of royal lineage, or will marry into royalty, or will become daughters of prime ministers, or women in prominent families, or daughters of great elders. They will be upright with perfect features. They will receive such blessings from having sincerely beheld and worshipped Earth Store Bodhisattva.

"Moreover, Universally Expansive, there may be good men or women who are able to play music, sing, or chant praises and make offerings of incense and flowers before images of the Bodhisattva, or who are able to exhort one or more others to do likewise. Now and in the future, such people will be surrounded day and night by hundreds of thousands of ghosts and spirits who will even prevent bad news from reaching their ears, much less allow them to be personally involved in any accidents.

"Moreover, Universally Expansive, in the future, evil people, evil spirits, or evil ghosts may see good men or women taking refuge with, respectfully making offerings to, praising, beholding, and bowing to images of Earth Store Bodhisattva. Those beings may ridicule and slander such acts of worship, saying that they are of no merit and benefit. They may sneer at those good people, condemn them behind their backs, or get a group or even one other person to have as little as one thought of condemnation. Such beings will fall into the Avichi Hell, and the extreme misery they will undergo as retribution for their slander will not end even after the thousand Buddhas of the Worthy Eon have passed into tranquility. Only after that eon will they be reborn among the hungry ghosts, where they will pass a thousand more eons before being reborn as animals. Only after another thousand eons will they obtain human bodies, but they will be poor and lowly with incomplete faculties, and their minds will be completely ensnared by their evil karma. Before long, they will fall into the evil paths again. Universally Expansive, such are the retributions that those who ridicule and slander others' acts of worship will undergo. How much worse will the retributions be if they cling to pernicious views as they engage in slander and destruction?

"Moreover, Universally Expansive, in the future, men or women may be bedridden for a long time and, in spite of their wishes, be unable either to get well or to die. At night they may dream of evil ghosts, or of family and relatives, or of wandering on dangerous paths. In numerous nightmares they may roam with ghosts and spirits. As days, months and years go by, such people may become weak and emaciated, cry out in pain in their sleep, and become progressively depressed and melancholy. Those things happen when the force of karma has not yet been determined, which makes it difficult for them to die and impossible for them to be cured. The ordinary eyes of men and women cannot perceive such phenomena.

"In that situation, other people should recite this sutra aloud once before images of the Buddhas and Bodhisattvas on behalf of any such sick person. Or they could offer to the Buddhas and Bodhisattvas possessions that the sick person cherishes, such as clothing, jewels, estates, or houses. They should speak distinctly to the sick person, saying, 'Now before this sutra or these images, we are offering these items on behalf of this sick person.' They may offer sutras or images, or commission images of Buddhas or Bodhisattvas, or build stupas or monasteries, or light oil lamps, or give to the Eternally Dwelling. They should tell the sick person three times about the offerings that are being made, making sure that the sick person both hears and understand what is being done.

"If the sick person's consciousnesses are already scattered and his or her breathing has stopped, then for one, two, three, four, and on through seven days, the other people should continue to inform the sick person clearly of the offerings and to read this sutra aloud. When such sick people's lives end, they will gain liberation from all the heavy and disastrous offenses committed in previous lives, even offenses warranting fivefold relentless retribution. They will be born in places where they will always know their past lives, so how much greater will the karmic rewards be if good men or good women can write out this sutra themselves or commission others to do so, or if they can carve or paint images themselves or commission others to do so. The benefits they receive will be great indeed!

"Therefore, Universally Expansive, if you see people reading and reciting this sutra or even having a single thought of praise or respect for it, you should employ hundreds of thousands of expedients to exhort such people to be diligent and not retreat. In both the present and the future, they will be able to obtain thousands of billions of inconceivable meritorious benefits.

"Moreover, Universally Expansive, beings in the future, while dreaming or drowsy, may see ghosts, spirits, and other forms that are either sad, weeping, or worried, fearful, or terrified. Those are all relatives such as fathers, mothers, sons, daughters, brothers, sisters, husbands, or wives from one, ten, a hundred, or a thousand lives past who have not yet been able to leave the bad destinies. They have nowhere to turn for the power of blessings needed to rescue them, and so they try to communicate with those who were their kin in previous lives, hoping that those relatives will use some skillful means to help them get out of the evil paths. Universally Expansive, using your spiritual power, exhort those relatives to recite this sutra with sincere resolve before the images of Buddhas or Bodhisattvas or to request others to recite it, either three or seven times. When the sutra has been read aloud the proper number of times, relatives in the evil paths will attain liberation and never again appear to those who are dreaming or drowsy.

"Moreover, Universally Expansive, people of low station, and those who are slaves, or servants, or deprived of their freedom in other ways, may be aware of their past deeds and wish to repent of them and to reform. If, while beholding and bowing to Earth Store Bodhisattva's image with sincere resolve for seven days, they are able to recite his name a full ten thousand times, then when their current retribution ends, those people will always be born into honorable families for hundreds of thousands of lives. How much more will they avoid any of the sufferings of the three evil paths.

"Moreover, Universally Expansive, in the future in Jambudvipa when the wives of Kshatriyas, Brahmans, Elders, and Upasakas of various families and clans are about to give birth to sons or daughters, the family members should recite this inconceivable sutra and recite the Bodhisattva's name a full ten thousand times during the seven days before the birth of those children. If those infants, whether male or female, were destined to undergo a terrible retribution for things done in past lives, they will be liberated from those retributions. They will be peaceful, happy, and easily raised, and their lives will be prolonged. If those children were due to receive blessings, then their peace and happiness will be increased, as will their life span.

"Moreover, Universally Expansive, in the future, on the first, eighth, fourteenth, fifteenth, eighteenth, twenty-third, twenty-fourth, twenty-eighth, twenty-ninth, and thirtieth days of the lunar month, the offenses of beings are tabulated and their gravity assessed. Every single movement or stirring of thought on the part of beings of Jambudvipa creates karma and offenses. How much more is that the case when they blatantly indulge in killing, stealing, sexual misconduct, false speech and hundreds of thousands of other kinds of offenses. If they are able to recite this sutra once on those ten days of purification, before the images of Buddhas, Bodhisattvas, or worthy ones and sages, then no disasters will occur within a radius of one hundred *yojanas* around them. The relatives of those who recite, both old and young, now and in the future, will be apart from the evil paths throughout hundreds of thousands of years. If they can recite this sutra once on each of these ten days of purification, then there will be no accidents or illnesses in the family, and they will have food and clothing in abundance.

"Therefore, Universally Expansive, you should know of the beneficial deeds done by Earth Store Bodhisattva as he makes use of his ineffable millions of billions of great awesome spiritual powers. The beings of Jambudvipa have strong affinities with this Great Lord. If they hear the Bodhisattva's name, see the Bodhisattva's image, or hear but a few words, a verse, or a sentence of this sutra, then they will enjoy particularly wonderful peace and happiness in this present life. Through thousands of millions of future lives, they will always be good-looking, and they will be born into honorable families."

Having heard the Buddha, Thus Come One, praise Earth Store Bodhisattva in that way, Universally Expansive Bodhisattva knelt, placed his palms together, and again addressed the Buddha, saying, "World Honored One, I have long known that this Great Lord has both inconceivable spiritual powers and mighty vows. I have questioned the Thus Come One so that beings in the future will know of these benefits. I now receive your answer most respectfully. World Honored One, what should the title of this sutra be, and how should we propagate it?"

The Buddha said to Universally Expansive, "This sutra has three titles: the first is *The Past Vows of Earth Store Bodhisattva*; it is also called *Earth Store's Past Conduct*; and also *Sutra of the Power of Earth Store's Past Vows*. Because this Bodhisattva repeatedly makes such great and mighty vows throughout long eons to benefit beings, you should all propagate this sutra in accordance with his vows."

After Universally Expansive had heard that, he placed his palms together respectfully, made obeisance, and withdrew.

CHAPTER VII

Benefiting the Living and the Dead

At that time, Earth Store Bodhisattva Mahasattva said to the Buddha, "World Honored One, I see that every single movement or stirring of thought on the part of beings of Jambudvipa is an offense. Beings tend to lose the wholesome benefits they accrue, and many of them end up retreating from their initial resolve. If they encounter evil conditions, they augment them with every thought. They are like people trying to carry heavy loads while walking through mud. Each step becomes more difficult and the loads more cumbersome as their feet sink deeper. If they meet a knowledgeable guide, he may be able to carry part or all of their burdens. This powerful mentor will aid them by advising them to tread carefully and to be mindful never to return to that treacherous path once they reach solid ground.

"World Honored One, beings who learn bad habits start from minor ones that soon grow to an immeasurable degree. Since all beings have such tendencies, their parents or relatives should create blessings for them when they are on the verge of dying in order to assist them on the road ahead. That may be done by hanging banners and canopies; lighting oil lamps; reciting the sacred sutras; making offerings before the images of Buddhas or sages; or just reciting the names of Buddhas, Bodhisattvas, and Pratyekabuddhas so that the recitation of each name passes by the ear of the dying one and is heard in his fundamental consciousness.

"Suppose the evil karma created by beings were such that they ought to fall into bad destinies. If their relatives cultivate wholesome causes on their behalf when they are close to death, then their manifold offenses can be dissolved. If relatives can further do many good deeds during the first forty-nine days after the death of such beings, then the deceased can leave the evil destinies forever, be born as humans and gods, and receive supremely wonderful bliss. The surviving relatives will also receive limitless benefits.

"Therefore, before the Buddhas, World Honored Ones, as well as before the gods, dragons, and the rest of the eightfold division, humans and non-humans, I now exhort beings of Jambudvipa to be careful to avoid harming, killing, and doing other unwholesome deeds; to refrain from worshipping ghosts and spirits or making sacrifices to them; and to never call on mountain sprites on the day of death. Why is that? Killing, harming, and making sacrifices do not even have a tiny hairsbreadth of power to benefit the deceased. Such acts only bind up the conditions of offenses so that they grow ever deeper and heavier. The deceased might have been due to increase his potential for sagehood or gain birth among humans or gods in his next life or in the future. But when his family commits offenses in his name, he will be burdened with defending himself, so his good rebirth will be delayed. How much more would that be the case for people on the verge of death who during their lives had failed to plant a few good roots? Each offender has to undergo the bad destinies according to his own karma. How could anyone bear to have relatives add to that karma? That would be like having a neighbor add a few more things to a load of over a hundred pounds being carried by someone who had already traveled a long distance and who had not eaten for three days. If that extra weight were added, that person's burden would become even more unbearable.

"World Honored One, I see that beings of Jambudvipa will themselves receive the benefit of any good deeds they are able to do within the Buddha's teachings. That holds true even when the deeds are as small as a strand of hair, a drop of water, a grain of sand, or a mote of dust."

After that had been said, an elder named Great Eloquence rose in the assembly. He had realized non-production long ago and was only appearing in the body of an elder to teach and transform those in the ten directions. Placing his palms together respectfully, he asked Earth Store Bodhisattva, "Great Lord, after people in Jambudvipa die and their young and old relatives cultivate merit by making vegetarian meal offerings and doing other such good deeds, will the deceased obtain merit and virtue significant enough to bring about their liberation?"

Earth Store replied, "Elder, based on the awesome power of the Buddhas, I will now expound this principle for the sake of beings of the present and future. Elder, if beings of the present and future, when on the verge of dying hear the name of one Buddha, one Bodhisattva, or one Pratyekabuddha, they will attain liberation whether they have committed offenses or not.

"When men or women laden with offenses who failed to plant good causes die, even they can receive one-seventh of any merit dedicated to them by young and old relatives who do good deeds on their behalf. The other six sevenths of the merit will accrue to the living relatives who did the good deeds. It follows that men and women of the present and future who cultivate while they are strong and healthy will receive all portions of the benefit derived.

"The arrival of the great ghost of Impermanence is so unexpected that the deceased ones' consciousnesses first drift in darkness, unaware of offenses and blessings. For forty-nine days the deceased are as if deluded or deaf, or as if in various courts where their karmic retributions are being decided. Once judgment is fixed, they are reborn according to their karma. In the time before rebirths are determined, the deceased suffer from thousands upon thousands of anxieties. How much more is that the case for those who are to fall into the bad destinies?

"Throughout forty-nine days, those whose lives have ended and who have not yet been reborn will be hoping every moment that their immediate relatives will earn blessings powerful enough to rescue them. At the end of that time, the deceased will undergo retribution according to their karma. If someone is an offender, he may pass through hundreds of thousands of years with no prospect of liberation. If someone's offenses deserve fivefold relentless retribution, he will fall into the great hells and undergo incessant suffering throughout hundreds of millions of eons.

"Moreover, Elder, when beings who have committed karmic offenses die, their relatives may prepare vegetarian offerings to aid them on their karmic paths. In the process of preparing the vegetarian meal and before it has been eaten, rice-washing water and vegetable leaves should not be thrown on the ground. Before the food is offered to the Buddhas and the Sangha, no one should eat it. If there is laxness or transgression in this matter, then the deceased will receive no strength from it. If purity is rigorously maintained in making the offering to the Buddhas and the Sangha, the deceased will receive one seventh of the merit. Therefore, Elder, by performing vegetarian offerings on behalf of deceased fathers, mothers, and other relatives while making earnest supplication on their behalf, beings of Jambudvipa benefit both the living and the dead."

After that was said, thousands of billions of *nayutas* of ghosts and spirits of Jambudvipa who were in the palace of the Trayastrimsha Heaven, made the unlimited resolve to attain Bodhi. The elder Great Eloquence made obeisance and withdrew.

CHAPTER VIII

Praises of King Yama and His Multitudes

At that time, from within the Iron Ring Mountain, King Yama and innumerable ghost kings came before the Buddha in the Trayastrimsha Heaven. They were: the ghost king Evil Poison, the ghost king Many Evils, the ghost king Great Argument, the ghost king White Tiger, the ghost king Blood Tiger, the ghost king Crimson Tiger, the ghost king Spreading Disaster, the ghost king Flying Body, the ghost king Lightning Flash, the ghost king Wolf Teeth, the ghost king Thousand Eyes, the ghost king Animal Eater, the ghost king Rock Bearer, the ghost king Lord of Bad News, the ghost king Lord of Calamities, the ghost king Lord of Food, the ghost king Lord of Wealth, the ghost king Lord of Domestic Animals, the ghost king Lord of Birds, the ghost king Lord of Beasts, the ghost king Lord of Mountain Sprites, the ghost king Lord of Birth, the ghost king Lord of Life, the ghost king Lord of Sickness, the ghost king Lord of Danger, the ghost king Three Eyes, the ghost king Four Eyes, the ghost king Five Eyes, the *Qi Li Shi* King, the Great *Qi Li* Shi King, the *Qi Li* Cha King, the Great *Qi Li* Cha King, the *No Cha* King, the Great *No Cha* King, and other such great ghost kings. With them were hundreds of thousands of minor ghost kings who dwelt throughout Jambudvipa, each presiding over certain jurisdictions.

Aided by the Buddha's awesome spiritual strength and the power of Earth Store Bodhisattva Mahasattva, all these ghost kings joined King Yama in the Trayastrimsha Heaven and together they stood to one side. Then King Yama knelt, placed his palms together, and said to the Buddha, "World Honored One, aided by the Buddha's awesome spiritual strength and the power of Earth Store Bodhisattva, I have been able to come here with all these ghost kings to join this great assembly in the Trayastrimsha Heaven, which will be very much to our benefit. There is now a small doubt that I should like to express, and we hope the World Honored One will be compassionate and resolve it."

The Buddha told King Yama, "I will answer any question you would like to ask."

At that time, King Yama gazed respectfully at the World Honored One, made obeisance, turned his head to acknowledge Earth Store Bodhisattva, and then said to the Buddha, "World Honored One, I observe that Earth Store Bodhisattva undaunted by fatigue, uses hundreds of thousands of expedient devices to rescue beings who are suffering for their offenses within the six paths of rebirth. Although this great Bodhisattva uses his inconceivable spiritual penetrations to do such deeds, it doesn't take long for the beings whom he has helped in gaining release from retribution to fall into the bad paths again.

"World Honored One, since Earth Store Bodhisattva has such great inconceivable spiritual power, why are beings not able to stay on the good paths, and be freed once and for all? Please, World Honored One, explain that for us."

The Buddha told King Yama, "The beings of Jambudvipa have stubborn and obstinate natures, difficult to tame, difficult to subdue. This great Bodhisattva continually rescues such beings throughout hundreds of thousands of eons, causing them to attain liberation quickly. For those beings undergoing retributions even in the worst destinies, the Bodhisattva applies the strength of expedients to extricate them from their own basic karmic conditions and leads them to understand the events of their past lives.

"But because beings of Jambudvipa are so bound up by their own heavy bad habits, they keep revolving in and out of the various paths over and over, as this Bodhisattva labors throughout many long eons to entirely effect their rescue and release.

"They are like people who, in confusion, lose their way home and take a dangerous road by mistake. On that dangerous road are many *yakshas*, tigers, wolves, lions, serpents, vipers, and scorpions. Those confused people are sure to be harmed very quickly on that dangerous path. But then they meet a knowledgeable guide, skilled in avoiding all the potential harm, including the toxins of the *yakshas* and others. This guide begins to lead the travelers off that dangerous path, saying, 'Beware, you fellows! What business has brought you onto this road? What kinds of special skills do you have to avoid all those dangers?'

"Hearing that, the confused travelers realize that they are on a dangerous path and turn back, attempting to escape. The kind guide then takes them by the hand and leads them off the dangerous path, steering clear of the deadly peril. When they reach a safe road, the travelers are relieved and happy. Their guide then says to them, 'Take care, confused ones; never get back on that path again after today. Once on it, it is hard to get off; you could lose your life.'

"The travelers who had lost their way express their deep gratitude, and as they are about to part, the guide says to them, 'If you see any relatives or other travelers, be they men or women, tell them of the dangers and evils on that path that could destroy their very natures and lives. Do not allow them to unwittingly bring about their own deaths.' In the same way, Earth Store Bodhisattva, replete with great compassion, rescues beings who are suffering for their offenses and enables them to be born among humans and gods, where they enjoy wonderful bliss.

"Once those offenders are released from the suffering they experienced in the paths where their karma took them, they must never go down those roads again. They are like the lost people who mistakenly took a dangerous path and were led to safety by a kind mentor. They know now to never take that road again. Moreover, they exhort others not to get on that road by saying, 'We took that road ourselves when we got confused, but we escaped and now we know better than to ever get on that road again. If we were to set foot on it again, it would be because we are still confused and did not recognize it as the dangerous path we took before. That being the case, we might lose our lives.' The same holds true for falling into the bad destinies. Due to the powerful expedient means of Earth Store Bodhisattva, beings can be freed and can gain rebirth as humans or gods. But soon they enter into the bad destinies again, and if their karmic bonds are heavy, they might remain in the hells forever with no chance of escape."

At that time, the ghost king Evil Poison placed his palms together respectfully, addressed the Buddha, and said, "World Honored One, each of us countless ghost kings of Jambudvipa bestows benefit or inflicts harm on beings differently. However, the karmic retributions of ghost kings cause those of our retinue to do more evil than good. Nonetheless, when we pass by a family residence, a city, a village, an estate, or a house where there are men or women who have cultivated as little as a hair's worth of good deeds, even if they have hung up but one banner or one canopy, used a little incense or a few flowers as offerings to images of Buddhas or Bodhisattvas, recited the sacred sutras or burned incense as an offering to even one sentence or gatha in them - we ghost kings will respect such people as we would the Buddhas of the past, present, and future. We will instruct the smaller ghosts, each of whom has great power, as well as the earth spirits, to protect such people. Bad situations, accidents, severe or unexpected illnesses, and all other unwelcome events will not even come near their residences or other places where they may be, much less enter the door."

The Buddha praised the ghost kings, "Excellent, excellent, that all of you ghost kings join King Yama in protecting good men and women in that way. I shall tell Lord Brahma and Lord Shakra to see that you are protected as well."

When that was said, a ghost king in the assembly named Lord of Life said to the Buddha, "World Honored One, my karmic conditions are such that I have jurisdiction over the life span of people in Jambudvipa, governing both the time of their births and their deaths. My fundamental vows are based on a great wish to benefit them, but people do not understand my intent and go through birth and death in distress. Why is that?

"When women in Jambudvipa have just given birth to children, be they boys or girls, or when they are just about to give birth, good deeds should be done to increase the benefits of the household, thus causing the local earth spirits to be immeasurably pleased. The spirits will then protect the mother and child so that they experience peace and happiness, and will bring benefit to the entire family. After the birth, all killing and injuring for the purpose of offering fresh meat to the mother should be carefully avoided, as should large family gathering that include drinking alcohol, eating meat, singing, and playing musical instruments. All those things can keep the mother and child from being peaceful and happy. Why is that? At the difficult time of birth, uncountable evil ghosts, mountain sprites, goblins, and spirits desire to eat the strong-smelling blood. Long in advance I order the local earth spirits of that household to protect the mother and child, allowing them to be peaceful and happy and to receive other benefits. When people in such households witness those benefits, they should do meritorious deeds to express their gratitude to the earth spirits. If instead, they harm and kill beings in order to host large family gatherings, then the retributions that result from such offenses will be borne by them and will bring harm to the mother and child as well.

"Moreover, when people of Jambudvipa are on the verge of death, I wish to keep them from falling into the evil paths, regardless of whether they have done good or evil. But how much is this power of mine to help them increased when they have personally cultivated good roots! When those who practice good in Jambudvipa are about to die, hundreds of thousands of ghosts and spirits from the evil paths transform themselves and appear as their parents or other relatives in an attempt to lead such people to fall into the evil paths. How much more is that the case for those who have done evil deeds?

"World Honored One, when men or women in Jambudvipa are on the verge of death, their consciousnesses are in a stupor. They are unable to discriminate between good and evil, and their eyes and ears are unable to see or hear. That is why relatives of those deceased people should make generous offerings, recite the sacred sutras, and recite the names of Buddhas and Bodhisattvas. Such good conditions can cause the deceased to leave the evil paths, and all the demons, ghosts, and spirits to withdraw and disperse.

"World Honored One, if at the time of death beings of any kind have an opportunity to hear the name of one Buddha or Bodhisattva or to hear a sentence or gatha of a Mahayana sutra, I observe that such beings can quickly be freed from the pull of their accumulated minor bad deeds that would otherwise send them to bad paths. The exception to that are the five offenses involving killing and harming that warrant relentless retribution."

The Buddha told the ghost king Lord of Life, "Because of your great compassion, you are able to make such great vows and protect all beings in the midst of life and death. When men or women in the future undergo birth and death, do not retreat from your vow, but liberate them all so that they can experience eternal peace."

The ghost king told the Buddha, "Please do not be concerned. Until the end of my life, in every thought I shall protect beings of Jambudvipa, both at the time of birth and of death, so that they all find tranquility. I only wish that at the time of birth and of death they would believe what I say, so that they can all be liberated and gain many benefits."

At that time, the Buddha told Earth Store Bodhisattva, "This great ghost king Lord of Life has already passed through hundreds of thousands of lives as a great ghost king, protecting beings during both birth and death. Only because of this Great Lord's compassionate vows does he appear in the body of a mighty ghost, for in reality he is not a ghost. After one hundred and seventy eons have passed, he will become a Buddha named Devoid of Attributes Thus Come One. His eon will be called Happiness, and his world will be named Pure Dwelling. That Buddha's

75

life will continue for incalculable eons. Earth Store, the circumstances surrounding this great ghost king are thus. They are inconceivable, and the people and gods whom he rescues are countless."

End of Part Two of

Sutra of the Past Vows of Earth Store Bodhisattva.

The True Words of Seven Buddhas for Eradicating Offenses

li po li po di, qiu he qiu he di, tuo luo ni di,
ni he la di, pi li ni di, mo he qie di,
zhen ling qian di, suo po he. (3x)

Spirit Mantra for Rebirth in the Pure Land

na mo e mi duo po ye, duo tuo qie duo ye,
duo di ye tuo, e mi li du po pi, e mi li duo,
xi dan po pi, e mi li duo, pi jia lan di,
e mi li duo, pi jia lan duo, qie mi li,
qie qie nuo, zhi duo jia li, suo po he. (3x)

Mantra for Patching the Flaws in Recitation

na mo he la da na, duo la ye ye,
qie la qie la, ju zhu ju zhu, mo la mo la,
hu la, hong, he he su da na, hong, po mo nu,
suo po he. (3x)

Praise

Universal Worthy requests; Earth Store replies in depth,

So that beings in the Three Paths and Six Realms go free;

From the dusty world of rebirths.

Universally Expansive asks the Tathagata,

And learns of Predictions and the Ten Fasting Days;

So that all reach the Lotus Terrace.

Homage to Earth Store Bodhisattva Mahasattva. (3x)

Earth Store Bodhisattva Praise

Earth Store Bodhisattva, wonderful beyond compare;

Gold-hued in his transformation body he appears.

Wondrous Dharma-sounds throughout the
    Three Paths and Six Realms;

Four Births and Ten Kinds of Beings gain his kindly grace.

His pearl, shining brightly, lights the way to heaven's halls;

Six-ringed golden staff shakes open wide the gates of hell.

Leads on those with causes garnered life and life again;

To bow at the Nine-flowered Terrace of
    the Honored One.

Namo Earth Store Great Vows and Compassion

Bodhisattva of the dark and dismal worlds;

On Nine Flower Mountain, Most Honored One,

With Ten Wheels of power you rescue all
    the suffering ones.

Homage to Earth Store Bodhisattva.
(Recite while circumambulating)

Part Three

of

Sutra of the Past Vows of Earth Store Bodhisattva

CHAPTER IX

The Names of Buddhas

At that time, Earth Store Bodhisattva Mahasattva said to the Buddha, "World Honored One, I will now describe some wholesome practices that will enable beings of the future to gain great benefit throughout their lives and deaths. World Honored One, please hear my words."

The Buddha told Earth Store Bodhisattva, "Now you wish to compassionately rescue all those in the six paths who are suffering for their offenses by discussing some inconceivable events. This is the right time. Speak now, since my Nirvana is near. You can then complete your vows soon. And I need not be worried about beings of the present or future."

Earth Store Bodhisattva said to the Buddha, "World Honored One, countless *asamkhyeya* eons ago, a Buddha named Boundless Body Thus Come One appeared in the world. If men or women hear this Buddha's name and have a momentary thought of respect, those people will overstep the heavy offenses involved in birth and death for forty eons. How much more will that be the case for those who sculpt or paint this Buddha's image or praise and make offerings to him? The blessings they reap will be limitless and unbounded.

"Furthermore, in the past, as many eons ago as there are grains of sand in the Ganges River, a Buddha named Jewel Nature Thus Come One appeared in the world. If men or women hear this Buddha's name and instantly decide to take refuge, those people will never retreat from the unsurpassed path.

"Furthermore, in the past, a Buddha named Padma Supreme Thus Come One appeared in the world. If men or women hear this Buddha's name as the sound of it passes by their ears, those people will be reborn one thousand times in the Six Desire Heavens. How much more will that be the case if those people sincerely recite the name of that Thus Come One?

"Furthermore, in the past, ineffable ineffable *asamkhyeya* eons ago, a Buddha named Lion's Roar Thus Come One appeared in the world. If men or women hear this Buddha's name and in a single thought take refuge, those people will encounter numberless Buddhas who will rub the crowns of their heads and bestow predictions of enlightenment upon them.

"Furthermore, in the past, a Buddha named Krakucchanda

appeared in the world. If men or women hear this Buddha's name and sincerely behold, worship, or praise him, those people will become Great Brahma Heaven kings in the assemblies of the thousand Buddhas of the Worthy Eon and will there receive superior predictions.

"Furthermore, in the past, a Buddha named Vipashyin appeared in the world. If men or women hear this Buddha's name, those people will eternally avoid falling into the evil paths, will always be born among people or gods, and will abide in supremely wonderful bliss.

"Furthermore, in the past, as many eons ago as there are grains of sand in limitless and countless Ganges Rivers, a Buddha named Jewel Victory Thus Come One appeared in the world. If men or women hear this Buddha's name, those people will never fall into the evil path and will always abide in the heavens, experiencing supremely wonderful bliss.

"Furthermore, in the past, a Buddha named Jeweled Appearance Thus Come One appeared in the world. If men or women hear this Buddha's name and give rise to a thought of respect, those people will soon attain the fruitions of arhatship.

"Furthermore, limitless *asamkhyeya* eons ago, a Buddha named Kashaya Banner Thus Come One appeared in the world. If men or women hear this Buddha's name, those people will overcome the offenses of birth and death for one hundred great eons.

"Furthermore, in the past, a Buddha named Great Penetration Mountain King Thus Come One appeared in the world. If men or women hear this Buddha's name, those people will encounter as many Buddhas as there are grains of sand in the Ganges. Those Buddhas will speak Dharma extensively for them, and they will certainly realize Bodhi.

"Furthermore, in the past, there were Buddhas named Pure Moon Buddha, Mountain King Buddha, Wisdom Victory Buddha, Pure Name King Buddha, Accomplished Wisdom Buddha, Unsurpassed Buddha, Wonderful Sound Buddha, Full Moon Buddha, Moon-Face Buddha, and an ineffable number of other Buddhas. World Honored One, beings of the present and future, both gods and humans, both male and female, can amass such limitless merit and virtue by reciting only one Buddha's name. How much more merit will they amass by reciting many names. Those beings will personally obtain great benefits in their lives and deaths and will never fall into the evil paths.

"When a person is on the brink of death, if even one family member should recite a Buddha's name aloud just once for the ailing person, the karmic retributions of that person who is about to die will be dissolved, except for relentless retribution resulting from the five offenses.

The five offenses warranting relentless retribution are so extremely heavy that those who commit them should not escape retribution for millions of eons. If, however, when the offender is about to die, someone recites the names of Buddhas on his or her behalf, then those offenses can gradually be dissolved. How much more will that be the case for beings who recite those names themselves? The merit they create will be limitless and will eradicate measureless offenses."

CHAPTER X

The Conditions and Comparative Merit and Virtue of Giving

At that time, Earth Store Bodhisattva Mahasattva, inspired by the Buddha's awesome spiritual strength, rose from his seat, knelt, placed his palms together and said to the Buddha, "World Honored One, I have observed beings within the paths of karma and compared their acts of giving. Some do a little and some do a lot. Some receive blessings for one life, some for ten lives, and some receive great blessings and benefit for hundreds or thousands of lives. Why is that? Please, World Honored One, explain that for us."

At that time, the Buddha told Earth Store Bodhisattva, "Here in this assembly in the palace of the Trayastrimsha Heaven, I will now discuss the comparative merit and virtue derived from acts of giving done by the beings in Jambudvipa. Listen attentively to what I say."

Earth Store said to the Buddha, "I have wondered about this matter and will be pleased to listen."

The Buddha told Earth Store Bodhisattva, "In Jambudvipa,

leaders of nations, prime ministers, high officials, great elders, great Kshatriyas, great Brahmans, and others may encounter those who are poor and disadvantaged, hunchbacked, physically challenged, impaired in speech, mute, deaf, retarded, blind, or disabled in other ways. Those national leaders and others may give to those unfortunate ones with great compassion, a humble heart, and a smile. They may give generously with their own hands or arrange for others to do so, comforting the recipients with gentle words. The blessings and benefits that such leaders and good people will accrue will be comparable to the meritorious virtue derived from giving to as many Buddhas as there are grains of sand in a hundred Ganges Rivers. Why is that? Those leaders and good people will receive such rewards of blessings and benefits for having shown a greatly compassionate heart toward the most impoverished, underprivileged, and physically challenged individuals. Throughout hundreds of thousands of lives to come, they will always have an abundance of the seven precious things, not to mention clothing, food, and the necessities of life.

"Moreover, Earth Store, in the future, the leaders of nations, Brahmans, and others may encounter Buddhist stupas or monasteries, or images of Buddhas, Bodhisattvas, Hearers, or Pratyekabuddhas and personally initiate and oversee the giving of offerings to them. If they do that, each of those leaders and good people will serve as Lord

Shakra for a duration of three eons, enjoying supremely wonderful bliss. If they are able to dedicate the blessings and benefits of that giving to the Dharma Realm, then those leaders of nations and good people will reign as great Brahma Heaven kings for ten eons.

"Moreover, Earth Store, in the future, leaders of nations, Brahmans, and others may, upon encountering ancient Buddhist stupas and monasteries or sutras and images that are damaged, decaying, or broken, resolve to restore them. Those leaders and good people may then oversee that task themselves, or encourage others to do so, gathering as many as hundreds of thousands of people to contribute and thereby establish affinities. Those leaders and good people will become wheel-turning kings for hundreds of thousands of successive lives, and those who made offerings with them will later be leaders of small nations for as many lives. If they resolve to dedicate that merit before the stupas or monasteries, then, based on that limitless and unbounded reward, those leaders, good people, and their helpers will eventually all complete the path to Buddhahood.

"Moreover, Earth Store, in the future, leaders of nations, Brahmans, and others may give rise to just one compassionate thought upon seeing the old, the sick, or women in childbirth, and provide them with medicine, food, drink, and bedding so as to make them peaceful and comfortable. The blessings and benefits derived from doing that are quite inconceivable. For one thousand eons they will always be lords of the Pure Dwelling Heavens, for two hundred eons they will be lords in the Six Desire Heavens, and they will ultimately attain Buddhahood. They will never fall into the evil paths, and for hundreds of thousands of lives they will hear no sounds of suffering.

"Moreover, Earth Store, if in the future, leaders of nations, Brahmans, and others can give in that way, they will receive limitless blessings. If, in addition, they are able to dedicate that merit, be it great or small, they will ultimately attain Buddhahood. How much more easily will they be able to attain the rewards of becoming Shakra, Brahma, or a wheel-turning king? Therefore, Earth Store, you should urge beings everywhere to learn to give in those ways.

"Moreover, Earth Store, in the future, if good men or good women only manage to plant a few good roots within the Buddhadharma, equivalent to no more than a strand of hair, a grain of sand, or a mote of dust, they will receive incomparable blessings and benefits.

"Moreover, Earth Store, in the future, good men or women, upon encountering images of Buddhas, Bodhisattvas, Pratyekabuddhas, or wheel-turning kings, may make offerings to them. Such persons will obtain limitless blessings and will always enjoy supremely wonderful bliss in the human and heavenly realms. If they can dedicate that merit to the Dharma Realm, their blessings and benefits will be beyond compare.

"Moreover, Earth Store, in the future, good men or good women, upon encountering Great Vehicle sutras or upon hearing but a single gatha or sentence of them, may be inspired to praise, venerate, and make offerings to them. Those people will obtain great limitless and unbounded rewards. If they can dedicate that merit to the Dharma Realm, their blessings will be beyond compare.

"Moreover, Earth Store, in the future, good men or good women may, upon encountering new Buddhist stupas, temples, or sutras of the Great Vehicle, make offerings to them, gaze at them in worship, and respectfully make praises with joined palms. Upon encountering old stupas, temples, or sutras, or those that have been destroyed or damaged, they may either do the repairing or rebuilding themselves or encourage others to help them. Those who help will become leaders of small nations for thirty successive lives. The donors themselves will always be wheel-turning kings who will use the good Dharma to teach and transform those leaders of small nations.

"Moreover, Earth Store, in the future, good men or good women may plant good roots in the Buddhadharma by giving, making offerings, repairing stupas or temples, rebinding sutras, or doing other good deeds amounting to no more than a strand of hair, a mote of dust, a grain of sand, or a drop of water. Merely by transferring the merit from such deeds to the Dharma Realm, those people will create merit and virtue that will enable them to enjoy superior and wonderful bliss for hundreds of thousands of lives. But if they dedicate the merit only to their families or to their own personal benefit, then they will enjoy just three lives of happiness. By giving up one, a ten-thousandfold reward is obtained. So it is, Earth Store. The circumstances pertaining to the causes and conditions of giving are thus."

CHAPTER XI

The Dharma Protection of an Earth Spirit

At that time, the earth spirit Firm and Stable addressed the Buddha thus, "World Honored One, since long ago I have personally beheld and bowed to limitless numbers of Bodhisattvas Mahasattvas. All of them have inconceivably great spiritual penetrations and wisdom that they use in taking across vast numbers of beings. Among all the Bodhisattvas, Earth Store Bodhisattva Mahasattva has the deepest and most weighty vows. World Honored One, Earth Store Bodhisattva has great affinities with beings in Jambudvipa. Likewise Manjushri, Samantabhadra, Contemplator of the World's Sounds, and Maitreya also manifest hundreds of thousands of transformation bodies to rescue those in the six paths, but their vows will ultimately be fulfilled. Earth Store Bodhisattva has made vows to teach and transform beings in the six paths throughout eons as numerous as sand grains in thousands of billions of Ganges Rivers.

"World Honored One, as I regard beings of the present and future, I see those who make shrines of clay, stone, bamboo, or wood and set them on pure ground in the southern part of their dwellings. They place within the shrines images of Earth Store Bodhisattva, either sculpted or painted, or made of gold, silver, copper, or iron. Then they burn incense, make offerings, behold, worship, and praise him. By doing those things, such people will receive ten kinds of benefits.

"What are these ten? First, their lands will be fertile. Second, their families and homes will always be peaceful. Third, their ancestors will be born in the heavens. Fourth, those still alive will increase their life span. Fifth, they will obtain what they seek. Sixth, they will not encounter disasters of water and fire. Seventh, they will avoid unforeseen calamities. Eighth, they will never have nightmares. Ninth, they will be protected by spirits in their daily comings and goings. Tenth, they will encounter many causes that lead to sagehood.

"World Honored One, beings of the present and future who make offerings in their homes in the prescribed manner will attain benefits like these."

The earth spirit further said to the Buddha, "World Honored One, good men or women in the future may keep this sutra and an image of the Bodhisattva where they live. Moreover, they may recite the sutra and make offerings to the Bodhisattva. I shall constantly use my own spiritual powers day and night to guard and protect those who do that from disasters, including floods, fire, robbery and theft, major disasters, and minor accidents."

The Buddha told the earth spirit Firm and Stable, "There are few spirits who can match your great spiritual power. Why do I say that? All the lands in Jambudvipa receive your protection. All the grasses, woods, sands, stones, paddy fields, hemp, bamboo, reeds, grains, rice, and gems come forth from the earth because of your power. Moreover, your constant praising of the beneficial deeds of Earth Store Bodhisattva makes your meritorious virtue and spiritual penetrations hundreds of thousands of times greater than those of other earth spirits.

"If good men or women in the future make offerings to this Bodhisattva, or recite *The Sutra of the Past Vows of Earth Store Bodhisattva* and rely upon even a single aspect of it in their cultivation, you should use your own spiritual powers to protect them. Do not allow any disasters or unwelcome events even to be heard, much less undergone, by them. Not only will those people be protected by you, but they will also be protected by the retinue of Shakra, Brahma, and other gods. Why will they receive protection from sages and worthies such as these? It will be due to their having beheld and worshipped an image of Earth Store Bodhisattva and from having recited this sutra of his past vows. Such people will quite naturally be able to leave the sea of suffering and will ultimately be certified to the bliss of Nirvana. For those reasons, they will receive great protection."

CHAPTER XII

Benefits Derived from Seeing
and Hearing

At that time, the World Honored One emitted hundreds of millions of billions of great rays of light from the crown of his head. They were the white ray, the great white ray, the auspicious ray, the great auspicious ray, the jade ray, the great jade ray, the purple ray, the great purple ray, the blue ray, the great blue ray, the azure ray, the great azure ray, the red ray, the great red ray, the green ray, the great green ray, the gold ray, the great gold ray, the celebration cloud ray, the great celebration cloud ray, the thousand-wheeled ray, the great thousand-wheeled ray, the jeweled wheel ray, the great jeweled wheel ray, the solar disc ray, the great solar disc ray, the lunar disc ray, the great lunar disc ray, the palace ray, the great palace ray, the ocean cloud ray, and the great ocean cloud ray.

After emitting such rays of light from the opening at the crown of his head, he spoke in subtle and wonderful sounds to the great assembly of gods, dragons, the rest of the eightfold division, humans, non-humans and others. "Hear me today in the palace of the Trayastrimsha

Heaven as I praise Earth Store Bodhisattva's beneficial and inconceivable deeds among humans and gods, his transcendent deeds that caused him to attain sagehood, his certification to the Tenth Ground, and his irreversibility from *Anuttarasamyaksambodhi.*"

After he said that, a Bodhisattva Mahasattva named Contemplator of the World's Sounds rose from his seat in the assembly, knelt on one knee, and with palms together said to the Buddha, "World Honored One, Earth Store Bodhisattva Mahasattva is replete with great compassion and pities beings who are suffering for their offenses. In thousands of billions of worlds he creates thousands of billions of transformation bodies through the strength of his meritorious virtue and inconceivable awesome spiritual power.

"I have heard the World Honored One and the numberless Buddhas of the ten directions praise Earth Store Bodhisattva in unison, saying that even if all the Buddhas of the past, present and future were to speak of his meritorious qualities, they could never finish describing them. Earlier, the World Honored One had told the great assembly that he wanted to praise Earth Store Bodhisattva's beneficial deeds and so forth. I now beseech the World Honored One to praise the inconceivable deeds of Earth Store Bodhisattva, for the sake of beings of the present and future and to cause the gods, dragons, and the rest of the eightfold division to gaze in worship and obtain blessings."

The Buddha replied to Contemplator of the World's Sounds Bodhisattva, "You have deep affinity with the Saha world. If gods, dragons, men, women, spirits, ghosts, or any other beings who are suffering for offenses within the six paths hear your name, see your image, behold you, or praise you, they will definitely become irreversible on the Unsurpassed Way. They will always be born in the realms of people and gods and there experience wonderful bliss. When the effects of their causes come to fruition, they will encounter Buddhas who will give them predictions. You are now replete with great compassion and pity for beings, for gods, dragons, and the rest of the eightfold division. Listen as I proclaim Earth Store Bodhisattva's inconceivable, beneficial deeds. Listen attentively, I will now talk about them."

The Contemplator of the World's Sounds said, "So be it, World Honored One, we will be pleased to listen."

The Buddha told the Bodhisattva Contemplator of the World's Sounds, "In worlds of the present and future, gods whose heavenly blessings are ending may be manifesting the five signs of decay, indicating that they may be about to fall into the evil paths. When those signs appear, if those gods, whether male or female, see Earth Store Bodhisattva's image or hear his name and gaze at him or bow but once to him, their heavenly blessings will thereby increase. They will experience great happiness and will never have to undergo retributions in the three evil paths. How much more will that be the case for those who, upon seeing and hearing the Bodhisattva, use incense, flowers, clothing, food, drink, jewels, and necklaces as offerings to him. The meritorious virtue, blessings, and benefits they gain will be limitless and unbounded.

"Moreover, Contemplator of the World's Sounds, in the worlds of the present and future, when beings in the six paths are on the verge of death, if they can hear the name of Earth Store Bodhisattva even once, such beings will never have to endure the sufferings of the three evil paths again. How much more will that be the case if the parents and other relatives use the houses, wealth, property, jewels, and clothing of such people who are on the verge of death to commission the carving or painting of images of Earth Store Bodhisattva. If those ailing people have not yet died, their relatives can try to help them see, hear, and understand that their houses, jewels, and so forth have been used for the carving or painting of images of Earth Store Bodhisattva on their behalf. If those people's karmic retributions were such that they were to undergo severe sickness, then, with such merit they can quickly be cured and their life span prolonged. If those people's retributions were to send them to the evil destinies at death due to their karma and obstacles, then with such merit they can, when their lives end, be born among people or gods and there enjoy extremely wonderful bliss. All their obstacles due to offenses will be eradicated.

"Moreover, Contemplator of the World's Sounds Bodhisattva, in the future, men or women may have lost their fathers, mothers, brothers, or sisters when they were still infants or as three-year-olds, five-year-olds, or youngsters under the age of ten. When they grow up, they may think about their deceased parents and other deceased relatives, not knowing into what paths or worlds or heavens they have been reborn. Suppose they are able to sculpt or paint images of Earth Store Bodhisattva or even to hear his name, gaze upon and worship him once and that, upon hearing his name and seeing his image, they gaze at him in worship and make offerings for one through seven days without retreating. If their deceased relatives had fallen into bad paths and were destined to remain there for many eons they would quickly gain release, be born among people or gods, and experience supreme bliss. This is because of their receiving the meritorious virtue generated by their sons, their daughters, their brothers or sisters, who sculpted or painted images of Earth Store Bodhisattva and then gazed upon and worshipped them.

"If such people's deceased relatives have already been born among people or gods on the strength of their own blessings and are already experiencing supreme bliss, then upon receiving that additional merit, their causes pertaining to sagehood will increase, and they will experience limitless bliss. If such people are able to behold and worship images of Earth Store Bodhisattva single-mindedly for three weeks, reciting his name a full ten thousand times, the Bodhisattva may then manifest a boundless body and describe to them the realms into which their deceased relatives have been born. Or in their dreams, the Bodhisattva may manifest great spiritual powers and personally lead them to those worlds to see their deceased relatives.

"Moreover, if they can recite the Bodhisattva's name one thousand times a day every day for one thousand days, the Bodhisattva will order the ghosts and earth spirits in their vicinity to guard and protect them for their entire lives. In this life their clothing and food will be abundant and they will have no suffering from sickness or other causes. No accidents will occur in their households, much less affect them personally. Finally, the Bodhisattva will rub the crowns of their heads and bestow predictions upon them.

"Moreover, Contemplator of the World's Sounds Bodhisattva, in the future, good men or women may want to practice great compassion in rescuing and taking across beings, may wish to cultivate unsurpassed Bodhi, and may long to leave the Triple World; and if those people see Earth Store Bodhisattva's image, hear his name, and sincerely take refuge with him; using incense, flowers, clothing, jewels, food and drink to make offerings while beholding and worshipping him; such good people's wishes will quickly be realized and they will never have any further obstructions.

"Moreover, Contemplator of the World's Sounds Bodhisattva, in the future, good men and women may want to fulfill millions of billions of vows and to succeed in as many undertakings both in the present and future. They need only take refuge with, gaze upon, worship, make offerings to, and praise the images of Earth Store Bodhisattva. In this way, their vows and aspirations can all be realized. Moreover, they may hope that Earth Store Bodhisattva, being endowed with great compassion, will always protect them; and in dreams the Bodhisattva will rub the crowns of their heads and bestow predictions upon them.

"Moreover, Contemplator of the World's Sounds Bodhisattva, in the future, good men and women may have high regard for the Great Vehicle sutras and make the inconceivable resolve to read and to recite them from memory. They may then encounter a brilliant master who instructs them so that they may become familiar with the texts; but as soon as they learn them, they forget them.

They may try for months or years and yet still be unable to read or recite them from memory. Because those good men and good women have karmic obstructions from past lives that have not yet been eradicated, they are unable to read and memorize sutras of the Great Vehicle. Upon hearing Earth Store Bodhisattva's name or seeing his image, such people should bring forth their true mind and, with deep respect and sincerity, state their situation to the Bodhisattva. In addition, they should use incense, flowers, clothing, food, and drink, and other beloved items as offerings to the Bodhisattva. They should place a bowl of clean water before the Bodhisattva for one day and one night. Afterwards, placing their palms together, they should state their request and then, while facing south, prepare to drink the water. As the water is about to enter their mouths, they should be particularly sincere and solemn. After drinking the water, they should abstain from the five pungent plants, wine, meat, improper sexual activity, false speech, and all killing and harming for one to three weeks. In dreams, those good men and women will then see Earth Store Bodhisattva manifest a boundless body and anoint the crowns of their heads with water. When they awaken, they will be endowed with keen intelligence, and upon hearing this sutra once, they will never forget or lose a single sentence or verse.

"Moreover, Contemplator of the World's Sounds Bodhisattva, in the future, there may be people whose food and clothing are insufficient, who find their efforts thwarted, who endure much sickness or misfortune, whose families are not peaceful, whose relatives are scattered, who are accident-prone, or who are often startled in their sleep by dreams. Upon hearing Earth Store's name and seeing his image, such people should recite his name a full ten thousand times with extreme sincerity and respect. Those inauspicious circumstances will gradually disappear, and they will find peace and happiness. Their food and clothing will be abundant, and even in their dreams they will be peaceful and happy.

"Moreover, Contemplator of the World's Sounds Bodhisattva, in the future, good men or women may have to enter mountain forests, cross rivers, seas, or other large bodies of water, or take dangerous routes either for the sake of earning their own livelihood, or for public or personal affairs, or matters of life and death, or other urgent business. Such people should first recite the name of Earth Store Bodhisattva a full ten thousand times. The ghosts and spirits of the lands they pass through will then guard and protect them whether they are walking, standing, sitting, or lying down. Those people will constantly be kept safe, so that even if they encounter tigers, wolves, lions, or any other harmful or poisonous creatures, they will not be harmed."

The Buddha told Contemplator of the World's Sounds

Bodhisattva, "Earth Store Bodhisattva has deep affinities with beings in Jambudvipa. Hundreds of thousands of eons would not be time enough to describe the benefits derived by beings who see this Bodhisattva and hear his name. Therefore, Contemplator of the World's Sounds Bodhisattva, you should use your spiritual powers to propagate this sutra, thus enabling beings in the Saha world to enjoy peace and happiness always, throughout hundreds of millions of eons."

At that time, the World-Honored One spoke in verses, saying:

I observe that Earth Store's awesome spiritual strength,
Could not be described in eons numerous as Ganges
    sands.
Seeing, hearing, beholding and bowing to him even once
Benefits people and gods in endless numbers of ways.

Men and women, gods and dragons, near the end
Of their rewards and doomed to fall into the evil paths
Can sincerely take refuge with this great being,
Thereby lengthening their lives and eradicating offenses.

Youngsters may lose their kind and loving parents,
And not know what paths their spirits are now on.

They may have lost brothers, sisters, and other kin,
Whom they never knew while growing up.

If they sculpt or paint this Great Lord's image,
Then with sorrowful longing, gaze at and bow to him
    unceasingly.
And for twenty one days recite his name,
The Bodhisattva will then display a boundless body,

And show them the realms where those kin were born,
Even if they've fallen into evil destinies, they will find
    escape.
If those praying can sustain their initial resolve,
The Bodhisattva may rub their heads and bestow
    predictions.

Those who wish to cultivate unsurpassed Bodhi
And leave behind the suffering of the Triple World,
Should give rise to the great compassionate heart.
First gaze and bow to this Great Being's image.
Every vow they make will soon be fulfilled,
And karmic obstructions will forever be halted.

Some people may resolve to read the sutra texts

Hoping to help those confused to reach the other shore.

Although the vows they make are inconceivable,

Try as they may, they cannot remember what they read.

Because of their karmic obstacles and delusions,

Those people cannot memorize the Mahayana sutras.

But, if they offer incense and flowers,

Clothing, food, and other cherished things to Earth
Store,

Place pure water on the Great Being's altar,

Pray for a day and night, then drink it,

Rigorously abstain from the five pungent plants,

Alcohol, meat, improper sex, and false speech,

For three weeks refrain from killing or hurting any
creature,

And, with utmost sincerity, be mindful of the name of
that Great Lord.

Then, in a dream, they will see his boundless body;

Upon awakening, they will have keen hearing.

After that, when they hear the teachings of the sutras,

They will never forget them for thousands of lives.

How inconceivable is this Great Lord
In helping those people gain such wisdom.

Beings who are impoverished or plagued with disease,
Whose homes are troubled; their relatives scattered,
Who find no peace even in sleep or dreams,
Whose efforts are thwarted, so wishes are unfulfilled,

May behold and bow to Earth Store's image with utmost
    sincerity.
All their evils deeds will then be eradicated.
Even dreams will become entirely peaceful.
Their food and clothing will be plentiful; spirits and
    ghosts will protect them.

Those who need to pass through mountain forests, or
    cross the seas,
Or go among poisonous or evil birds and beasts, or evil
    people,
Among evil spirits, evil ghosts, and even evil winds,
Or other dangerous and distressing situations,

Need only gaze in worship and make offerings
To an image of the Great Lord, Earth Store Bodhisattva.

Thereby, all evil in the mountain forests
And on the vast seas will disappear.

Contemplator of the World's Sounds, listen well to what
I say.
Earth Store Bodhisattva is eternal and unconceivable!
Hundreds of millions of eons is time too brief
To describe fully the powers of this Great Lord.

If people can but hear the name "Earth Store,"
Or see his image, or behold and bow to it;
Offer incense, flowers, clothing, food, and drink;
Their joy will last for hundreds of thousands of eons.

If they can dedicate such merit to the Dharma Realm,
They will become Buddhas, ending birth and death.
Contemplator of the World's Sounds, know this well,
And tell everyone everywhere in lands as many as
Ganges' sands.

CHAPTER XIII

The Entrustment of People and Gods

At that time, the World Honored One extended his gold-colored arm, and again rubbed the crown of the head of Earth Store Bodhisattva Mahasattva, saying, "Earth Store, Earth Store, your spiritual powers, compassion, wisdom, and eloquence are inconceivable. Even if all the Buddhas of the ten directions were to proclaim their praises of your inconceivable deeds, they could not finish in thousands of millions of eons.

"Earth Store, Earth Store, remember this entrustment that I am again making here in the Trayastrimsha Heaven in this great assembly of ineffable ineffable millions of billions of Buddhas, Bodhisattvas, gods, dragons, and the rest of the eightfold division. I again entrust to you the gods, people, and others who are still in the burning house and have not yet left the Triple World. Do not allow those beings to fall into the evil destinies even for a single day and night, much less fall into the fivefold Relentless Hell or the Avichi Hell, where they would have to pass through thousands of billions of eons with no chance of escape.

"Earth Store, the beings of southern Jambudvipa have irresolute wills and natures, and those who learn evil ways are many. Even if they resolve to do good, they soon renounce that resolve. If they encounter evil conditions, they become increasingly involved in them with every thought. For those reasons, I reduplicate hundreds of billions of bodies to transform beings, take them across, and liberate them, all in accord with their own basic dispositions.

"Earth Store, I now earnestly entrust the multitudes of gods and people to you. If in the future, there are gods and good men or women who plant a few good roots in the Buddhadharma, be they as little as a strand of hair, a mote of dust, a grain of sand, or a drop of water, then you should use your powers in the Way to protect them so that they gradually cultivate the unsurpassed Way and do not retreat from it.

"Moreover, Earth Store, in the future, gods or people, according to the responses of their karmic retributions, may be due to fall into the evil destinies. While they are on the brink of falling or already at the very gates to those paths, if they can recite the name of one Buddha or Bodhisattva or a single sentence or verse of a Great Vehicle sutra, then you should use your spiritual powers to rescue them with expedient means. Display a boundless body in the places where they are, smash the hells, and lead them to be born in the heavens and to experience supreme bliss."

At that time, the World Honored One spoke in verse, saying:

> I am entrusting to your care the multitudes
> Of gods and people both now and in the future.
> Use your great spiritual powers and expedients to save them.
> Do not allow them to fall into the evil destinies.

At that time, Earth Store Bodhisattva Mahasattva knelt on one knee, placed his palms together, and said to the Buddha, "I beg the World Honored One not to be concerned. In the future, if good men and women have a single thought of respect toward the Buddhadharma, I shall use hundreds of thousands of expedients to take them across and free them. They will quickly be liberated from birth and death. How much more will that be the case for those who, having heard about all these good undertakings, are inspired to cultivate. Those people will naturally become irreversible from the unsurpassed Way."

After he finished speaking, a Bodhisattva named Empty Space Treasury who was in the assembly spoke to the Buddha, "World Honored One, I personally have come to the Trayastrimsha Heaven and have heard the Thus Come One praise Earth Store Bodhisattva's inconceivable awesome spiritual power. If in the future, good men, good women, gods and dragons hear this sutra and the name of Earth Store Bodhisattva, and if they behold and bow to his image, how many kinds of blessings and benefits will they obtain? Please, World Honored One, say a few words about this for the sake of beings of the present and future."

The Buddha told Empty Space Treasury Bodhisattva, "Listen attentively, listen attentively. I shall enumerate them and describe them to you. In the future, if good men or women see Earth Store Bodhisattva's image, hear this sutra, read or recite it, and even use incense, flowers, food and drink, clothing, or precious things as offerings, praise, behold and bow to him, such beings will benefit in twenty-eight ways:

First, they will be protected by gods and dragons.

Second, their good roots will increase daily.

Third, they will amass supreme causes pertaining to sagehood.

Fourth, they will not retreat from Bodhi.

Fifth, their clothing and food will be abundant.

Sixth, they will never be affected by epidemics.

Seventh, they will not encounter disasters of fire and water.

Eighth, they will never be threatened by thieves.

Ninth, they will be respected by all who see them.

Tenth, they will be aided by ghosts and spirits.

Eleventh, women who want to can be reborn as men.

Twelfth, if born as women, they will be daughters of national leaders and officials.

Thirteenth, they will have upright and handsome features.

Fourteenth, they will often be born in the heavens.

Fifteenth, they may be emperors or leaders of nations.

Sixteenth, they will have the wisdom to know past lives.

Seventeenth, they will attain whatever they seek.

Eighteenth, their families will be happy.

Nineteenth, they will never undergo any disasters.

Twentieth, they will leave the bad karmic paths forever.

Twenty-first, they will always arrive at their destination.

Twenty-second, their dreams will be peaceful and happy.

Twenty-third, their deceased relatives will leave suffering behind.

Twenty-fourth, they will enjoy blessings earned in previous lives.

Twenty-fifth, they will be praised by sages.

Twenty-sixth, they will be intelligent and have keen faculties.

Twenty-seventh, they will be magnanimous, kind and empathetic.

Twenty-eighth, they will ultimately realize Buddhahood.

"Moreover, Empty Space Treasury Bodhisattva, if gods, dragons, or spirits of the present or future hear Earth Store's name, bow to Earth Store's image, or hear of Earth Store's past vows, deeds and practices, and then praise him, behold, and bow to him, they will benefit in seven ways:

First, they will quickly transcend to levels of sagehood.

Second, their evil karma will be eradicated.

Third, all Buddhas will protect and be near them.

Fourth, they will not retreat from Bodhi.

Fifth, their inherent powers will increase.

Sixth, they will know past lives.

Seventh, they will ultimately realize Buddhahood.

At that time, all the ineffable ineffable numbers of Buddhas, Thus Come Ones, who had come from the ten directions, the great Bodhisattvas, gods, dragons, and the rest of the eightfold division, having heard Shakyamuni Buddha's praise of Earth Store Bodhisattva's awesome and inconceivable spiritual powers, praised this unprecedented event. Following that, incense, flowers, heavenly garments, and pearl necklaces rained down in the Trayastrimsha Heaven as offerings to Shakyamuni Buddha and Earth Store Bodhisattva. After that, all the assembled beings gazed upwards, bowed, placed their palms together and withdrew.

End of Part Three of

Sutra of the Past Vows of Earth Store Bodhisattva.

The True Words of Seven Buddhas for Eradicating Offenses

li po li po di, qiu he qiu he di, tuo luo ni di,
ni he la di, pi li ni di, mo he qie di,
zhen ling qian di, suo po he. (3x)

Spirit Mantra for Rebirth in the Pure Land

na mo e mi duo po ye, duo tuo qie duo ye,
duo di ye tuo, e mi li du po pi, e mi li duo,
xi dan po pi, e mi li duo, pi jia lan di,
e mi li duo, pi jia lan duo, qie mi li,
qie qie nuo, zhi duo jia li, suo po he. (3x)

Mantra for Patching the Flaws in Recitation

na mo he la da na, duo la ye ye,
qie la qie la, ju zhu ju zhu, mo la mo la,
hu la, hong, he he su da na, hong, po mo nu,
suo po he. (3x)

Praise

Earth Store's basic vows and comparative causes of
  virtue are told.

We learn that crippling illness, physical defects, come
  from past lives' deeds.

In this life, those who recite Great Vehicle Sutras,

Bring benefits without end, aiding all
    to be reborn from jeweled lotuses.

Homage to Earth Store Bodhisattva Mahasattva. (3x)

Earth Store Bodhisattva Praise

Earth Store Bodhisattva, wonderful beyond compare;

Gold-hued in his transformation body he appears.

Wondrous Dharma-sounds throughout the
 Three Paths and Six Realms;

Four Births and Ten Kinds of Beings gain his kindly grace.

His pearl, shining brightly, lights the way to heaven's halls;

Six-ringed golden staff shakes open wide the gates of hell.

Leads on those with causes garnered life and life again;

To bow at the Nine-flowered Terrace of
 the Honored One.

Namo Earth Store Great Vows and Compassion

Bodhisattva of the dark and dismal worlds;

On Nine Flower Mountain, Most Honored One,

With Ten Wheels of power you rescue all
 the suffering ones.

Homage to Earth Store Bodhisattva.
(Recite while circumambulating)

Verse of Transference

May the merit and virtue accrued from this work,

Adorn the Buddhas' Pure Lands,

Repaying four kinds of kindness above,

And aiding those suffering in the paths below.

May those who see and hear of this,

All bring forth the resolve for Bodhi,

And when this retribution body is over,

Be born together in the Land of Ultimate Bliss.

Dharma Protector Wei Tuo Bodhisattva

Dharma Realm Buddhist Association Branches

World Headquarters

The City of Ten Thousand Buddhas
2001 Talmage Road
Ukiah, CA 95482 USA
tel: (707) 462-0939
fax: (707) 462-0949
www.drba.org
(Branch URLs and email addresses are available on the DRBA website.)

U.S.A.
California
Berkeley

Berkeley Buddhist Monastery
2304 McKinley Avenue
Berkeley, CA 94703 USA
tel: (510) 848-3440
fax: (510) 548-4551

Burlingame

The International Translation Institute
1777 Murchison Drive
Burlingame, CA 94010-4504 USA
tel: (650) 692-5912
fax: (650) 692-5056

Long Beach

Blessings, Prosperity, and Longevity Monastery
4140 Long Beach Boulevard
Long Beach, CA 90807 USA
tel/fax: (562) 595-4966

Long Beach Sagely Monastery
3361 East Ocean Boulevard
Long Beach, CA 90803 USA
tel: (562) 438-8902

Los Angeles

Gold Wheel Monastery
235 North Avenue 58
Los Angeles, CA 90042 USA
tel: (323) 258-6668
fax: (323) 258-3619

Sacramento

The City of the Dharma Realm
1029 West Capitol Avenue
West Sacramento, CA 95691 USA
tel: (916) 374-8268
fax: (916) 374-8234

San Francisco

Gold Mountain Monastery
800 Sacramento Street
San Francisco, CA 94108 USA
tel: (415) 421-6117
fax: (415) 788-6001

San Jose

Gold Sage Monastery
11455 Clayton Road
San Jose, CA 95127 USA
tel: (408) 923-7243
fax: (408) 923-1064

Maryland
Bethesda

Avatamsaka Vihara
9601 Seven Locks Road
Bethesda, MD 20817-9997 USA
tel/fax: (301) 469-8300

Washington
Index

Snow Mountain Monastery
PO Box 272
50924 Index-Galena Road
Index, WA 98256 USA
tel: (360) 799-0699
fax: (815) 346-9141

Seattle

Gold Summit Monastery
233 1st Avenue
West Seattle, WA 98119 USA
tel: (206) 284-6690

Canada
Alberta

Avatamsaka Monastery
1009 4th Avenue
S.W. Calgary, AB T2P OK, Canada
tel: (403) 234-0644

British Columbia

Gold Buddha Monastery
248 East 11th Avenue
Vancouver, B.C. V5T 2C3, Canada
tel: (604) 709-0248
fax: (604) 684-3754

Australia

Gold Coast Dharma Realm
106 Bonogin Road
Bonogin, Queensland AU 4213
Australia
tel: 61-755-228-788
fax: 61-755-227-822

Hong Kong

Buddhist Lecture Hall
31 Wong Nei Chong Road, Top Floor
Happy Valley, Hong Kong, China
tel: (852) 2572-7644
fax: (852) 2572-2850

Cixing Chan Monastery
Lantou Island, Man Cheung Po
Hong Kong, China
tel: (852) 2985-5159

Malaysia

Dharma Realm Guanyin Sagely Monastery
Prajna Guanyin Sagely Monastery
161, Jalan Ampang
50450 Kuala Lumpur, Malaysia
tel: (603) 2164-8055
fax: (603) 2163-7118

Fa Yuan Monastery
1 Jalan Utama
Taman Serdang Raya
43300 Seri Kembangan
Selangor Darul Ehsan, Malaysia
tel: (603) 8948-5688

Malaysia DRBA Penang Branch
32-32C, Jalan Tan Sri Teh Ewe Lim
11600 Jelutong
Penang, Malaysia
tel: (604) 281-7728
fax: (604) 281-7798

Guan Yin Sagely Monastery
166A Jalan Temiang
70200 Seremban
Negeri Sembilan, Malaysia
tel/fax: (606)761-1988

Lotus Vihara
136, Jalan Sekolah
45600 Batang Berjuntai
Selangor, Malaysia
tel: (603) 3271- 9439

Taiwan

Dharma Realm Buddhist Books Distribution Society
11th Floor, 85 Zhongxiao E. Road, Sec. 6
Taipei 115, Taiwan R.O.C.
tel: (02) 2786-3022
fax: (02) 2786-2674

Dharma Realm Sagely Monastery
No. 20, Dongxi Shanzhuang
Liugui Dist.
Gaoxiong 844, Taiwan, R.O.C.
tel: (07) 689-3717
fax: (07) 689-3870

Amitabha Monastery
No. 136, Fuji Street, Chinan Village, Shoufeng
Hualian County 974, Taiwan, R.O.C.
tel: (03) 865-1956
fax: (03) 865-3426

Subsidiary Organizations

Buddhist Text Translation Society
City of Ten Thousand Buddhas
4951 Bodhi Way, Ukiah. CA 95482 USA
web: www.buddhisttexts.org
email: info@buddhisttexts.org
catalog: www.bttsonline.org

Dharma Realm Buddhist University
City of Ten Thousand Buddhas
4951 Bodhi Way, Ukiah, CA 95482 USA
www.drbu.org

Dharma Realm Outreach
City of Ten Thousand Buddhas
outreach@drba.org

Instilling Goodness and Developing Virtue School
City of Ten Thousand Buddhas
2001 Talmage Road, Ukiah, CA 95482 USA
www.igdvs.org

Institute for World Religions
2245 McKinley Avenue, Suite B
Berkeley, CA 94703 USA
web: www.drbu.org/iwr
email: iwr@drbu.org

Religion East & West (journal)
2245 McKinley Avenue, Suite B
Berkeley, CA 94703 USA
tel: 510-848-9788
web: www.drbu.org/iwr/rew

Vajra Bodhi Sea (magazine)
Gold Mountain Monastery
800 Sacramento Street
San Francisco, CA 94108 USA
tel: (415) 421-6117
fax: (415) 788-6001